Joshua's Tree

Understanding God's Sovereign Order

by
Apostle David Allen &
Apostle Bill Yoho

Written by David Allen and Bill Yoho 2023
Joshua's Tree: Understanding God's Sovereign Order

ISBN: 978-1-7375902-3-1
Library of Congress Control Number: 2023923247 Printed in the United States of America

Scriptures marked KJV are taken from the KING JAMES VERSION (KJV): KING JAMES VERSION, public domain.
Scripture quotations taken from the Amplified® Bible (AMP), Copyright © 2015 by The Lockman Foundation. Used by permission. lockman.org
Scripture quotations taken from the (NASB®) New American Standard Bible®, Copyright © 1960, 1971, 1977, 1995, 2020 by The Lockman Foundation. Used by permission. All rights reserved. lockman.org

Candace Monroe Publishing
P. O. Box 310
Lumberton, NC 28359
www.candacejoyner.com

Joshua's Tree: Understanding God's Sovereign Order/David Allen and Bill Yoho

Table of Contents

The *Joshua Tree* and its ability to grow amongst harsh and unforgiving terrain, have long been a symbol of faith for thriving amidst adversity. It is seen as a symbol of *Love, Hope, and Faith,* reminding us that beauty and life can still flourish in the most challenging of times and environments.

Even as Joshua's Tree stands in a harsh environment, so is The Cluster placed in a hostile world, but as a corporate man, we prosper in the Kingdom of God as well.

Isaiah 65:8-10 KJV

8 Thus saith the LORD, As the new wine is found in the cluster, and one saith, Destroy it not; for a blessing is in it: so will I do for my servants' sakes, that I may not destroy them all.

9 And I will bring forth a seed out of Jacob, and out of Judah an inheritor of my mountains: and mine elect shall inherit it, and my servants shall dwell there.

10 And Sharon shall be a fold of flocks, and the valley of Achor a place for the herds to lie down in, for my people that have sought me.

But in the last of these days, He has spoken to us in [the person of a] Son, Whom He appointed Heir and lawful Owner of all things, also by and through Whom He created the worlds and the reaches of space and the ages of time [He made, produced, built, operated, and arranged them in order].

Hebrews 1:2 (AMP)

FOREWORD

The church presently is in a time of critical transition. God is changing the old order to the order that is to come. That order is brought forth through the Apostolic and Prophetic offices being restored to the church. Church order is a critical and vital part of healthy church growth and function.

Throughout history, every move of God, has brought forth change and a greater revelation of the present church. In this last day and hour God once again is bringing revelation to His church for change. The present-day order, which we will call the *Saul order*, brings death and woundedness to the body he loves so much.

This order is a Kingly order, not a shepherd order or role. We see this example in 1 Chronicles 15:7-12, when David tries to bring in the Ark, (or the presence of God) upon a new cart made of board and big wheels, which brought forth death when it hit the shaking. The religious carts of the church world are coming to the place of shaking. To the ones who are Legalist and Dogmatic, who are religious and who feel that the presence of God can be pulled or pushed or carried upon boards and big wheels, are coming to an understanding that the presence of God cannot be pushed, pulled, or steadied by man.

This is especially true for spirit filled churches. We must understand, like David, who finally came into the realization in 1 Chronicles 15:7, that God cannot be pushed, pulled, or even steadied by the hand of man. His presence is to be carried.

When David came into his present truth, he realized that by the Levites carrying the Ark of the Covenant upon their shoulders, that the presence of God and the Glory of God could be handled and brought into a place where all the people could be blessed. (Note: *the* <u>shoulders</u> *speak of Government*)

Once the proper government order is brought back into the church and the five-fold ministry offices are recognized and fully restored. God's presence is free to move with a greater revelation of the new wine that He wants to pour upon His church. The cluster found in Isaiah 65:8 reveals the revelation of this order.

It is my desire that this manual will instruct the Body and give clear insight to the revelation of the five-fold ministry and how it operates within the congregation of the Lord. In addition to the five-fold ministry, we will be discussing the Helps and Governments of the seven-fold ministry.

These two ministries are mentioned in **1 Corinthians 12:28**, *"and in the church God has appointed first apostle, second prophets, third teachers, then workers of miracles, also those having gifts of healing, those able to help others, those with gifts of administration, and those speaking in different kinds of tongues,"*

Right after miracles and gifts of healing, they are important work to the Church. God is bringing a new order for a new move, but let's remember that new wine must be put into new bottles and both are preserved (**Luke 5:38**).

Transition is sometimes difficult, because it requires humility and a willingness to make sacrifices. God will give grace to us to make the change, but remember no man having drunk the old wine straightway desires the new, for the old he says is better.

People must develop an appetite for the new wine. Once people hear and fully understand what God is doing in this hour through the Apostolic Church, they will begin to develop a taste and an appetite for the new wine. The diet of continually hearing the same old message from the past; It is time for change. Change comes by the Apostolic office laying down foundational truths as they establish the body and solidify peoples walk with the Lord. When we say that we must once again, in the Apostolic Church, re-lay foundations, it is because the previous foundation of the church will not be sufficient to build upon or expand.

A new foundation of truth must be laid for the church.

Isaiah 54:2, *"Enlarge the place of thy tent, and let them stretch forth the curtains of thine habitations: spare not, lengthen thy cords and strengthen thy stakes. For thou shalt break forth on the right hand and on the left: and thy seed shall inherit the Gentiles, and make the desolate cities to be inhabited."*

The foundation based on the present truth must be put into the hearts and minds of the believers. We must teach! Teaching is so important because people will not be able to make the shift or the transition unless we shift or change their mindsets. Most people have been trained to teach a certain way, for instance, most people still feel that the Pastoral order in the church is the Governing Head; this is a false teaching.

For many pastors run, control, and operate churches. We must change the mindsets that have been set in place for hundreds of years. The pastor is expected to preach, counsel, marry, bury, do all administration, oversee the church, and even sweep, clean, wait on tables, etc., this is not true, but the believer has been trained to think so. The apostolic mentality is quite different though; the leaders are to be released into their function.

Government order is to be set in place by the apostolic and the prophetic; thereby releasing the pastors into the role of an overseer, and not into the ministry of Helps or Administration.

We will see this as we progress into present day truths that are laid down for the local congregations. In the apostolic church, the governing gifts of the: apostle, prophets and teachers are set into place, the overseeing gifts of the pastor and the outreach gifts of the evangelist are released. The people learn to draw from all these gifts, and not to depend only upon the senior pastor for all their needs.

The minds of the people must be renewed, if they are to accept and embrace God's present new order of ministry. They must be taught that this is God's Order. Much of what the church has learned; has come through religion and man's order and tradition and not by revelation knowledge. We are seeing a radical change in this concept within the church world. Reformation always calls forth and requires restructuring and teaching on the thought patterns of the people.

The people are not able to handle such change, as long as they are bound in their thought patterns by religious mindsets and dogmatic thinking of men. The leaders such as the apostles, prophets, and teachers, must spend time, training the people for the new truths, so that the whole entire church might make a transition into the new order.

Teaching helps release the apostolic office and gifts within the local church. Teaching also gives us foundation to build on. Once people are convinced that what we are trying to do is scriptural, they will embrace what we are trying to do and back it 100%, because of their understanding of God's Word and presents truths.

Teaching causes people to begin to operate in faith and truth, and we know that truth sets us free. The people, God's people, will always come; but as I said earlier, change is painful and very difficult for some to make. For that reason; in this hour, my personal belief is that many people have a hard time releasing the things of the past and stepping into the new.

Alongside the apostolic teaching to bring forth the Reformation, we must understand that **1 Corinthians 12:28** speaks of the prophetic office which is even ahead of teachers and second to the apostolic. We must never let the prophetic ministry overshadow the apostolic ministry, but should work hand-in-hand with the apostolic ministry.

We see in **Ephesians 2:20** that the church is built upon the foundation of the apostolic and the prophetic. In this last hour, we see that God has raised up many prophetic churches to activate and to equip the Body of Christ that they might move in the prophetic gifts. But the prophetic gift can never be the dominate gift in the church; if it does it will become off balance. We saw this in our own congregation, when the Lord instructed me to take off the words "prophetic ministry" from our sign outside.

Chapter 1

How Do We Make It Through The Transition Safely?

First, inlets are often rough, so make sure everything is in its proper place or it may fall overboard or break. It is in the inlet of transition that God most targets our unconscious areas of pride, self-love, self-reliance, and counterfeit affections.

Areas of fleshy wisdom, that God's grace previously covered, will be exposed in greater degrees. Over and over, we may find our own ideas, opinions, and thoughts. Even a strong will can lie hidden behind even the gentlest of voices. These "presumptuous sins" must be brought to the light and dealt with before we break forth into to ocean and find deeper rest in the Father's love **(Psalm 19:12-14)**.

Secondly, traversing an inlet requires your greatest focus. Nothing brings our spirit man into focus more quickly than prolonged prayer and fasting. This is perhaps the greatest time in history when Christians most intense battlegrounds, especially leaders, will be in the realm of the soul.

"Is it a fast like this which I choose, a day for a man to humble himself.. to loosen the bonds of wickedness... and break every yoke?" **(Isaiah 58:5,6)**. This will be a year when greater grace will be given in the realm of prayer and fasting. Fasting eliminates our selfishness. Its fire purifies our hearts; its flames separate the base impurities from our real nature in Christ. I really think that there are some things that God wants us to have, but we

will never be able to have them unless we fast and pray together. We can never let someone's judgment or personal opinion's and feeling influences or shape our personal relationship with the Lord.

Thirdly, safely crossing rough inlets requires a quiet confidence and dependence upon skills learned in past experiences at sea. There can be no fear, or you panic at the crisis moment. I speak daily to many ministers from around the world who are in the midst of the river of God. Many are tired and weary. This is the place where dependence upon the Father is easily lost as the weariness leads to anxieties and insecurities and faith diminishes. My wife and I are in the best place we have ever been, relationally and spiritually, yet we hear God calling us into a deeper rest.

Therefore, we plan on taking three months this year where we minister to no one and aren't preparing for the next sermon. We just want to grow more secure in resting in our Father's love and spend time playing with Him as His little children. We know it will be preparation for us entering into deeper realms of glory that lie ahead.

Fourthly, of the inlet of transition, we must learn to "wait" on God in rougher inlets. You have to sit and wait on the larger swells to pass and look for an opening when you can get safely across the bar. I've seen an impatient captain try to rush through and the swells lift the vessel high and made it fall, slamming their propellers into the sand. They are left helpless, without power; the journey aborted as they are towed back to port.

When we wait extended periods on God, He acts on our behalf. Every few months, I try to enter into solitude and just sit all day and wait for God to come and renew my strength. He reveals His wonders during these seasons of waiting. If we act without waiting on God, then He waits on us to enter His rest before He acts. It is in the waiting that our strength is renewed and God's power increases **(Isaiah 30:18; 40:29-31; 64:4)**.

Charles Swindoll best described the posture that the father is calling us to in the inlet of transition:

- Simplicity
- Solitude
- Silence
- Submission

This year is a time of preparation for the outpouring of His wondrous love to a lost world. We are to simplify our lives and ministries by spending seasons separating ourselves from all the voices of need for the purpose of waiting on the Father.

Waiting is a sign of absolute dependence and submission. There is no more valuable time spent in the day than the time spent waiting on God! This is the position we experience the displacement of self by the enthronement of God. This is the place of humility where God is all and self becomes nothing. Our hearts are being prepared for the boundless ocean of His love that lies ahead.

Three things have developed: the world does not understand the prophetic ministry, the church is just coming into the understanding of the prophetic ministry, and the prophetic ministry cannot overshadow the Apostolic church. The apostolic church is the primary and main function of the church today. I am in no means trying to minimize the importance of the prophetic ministry, as well as the pastoral and evangelistic ministries to properly function. Nevertheless, we are now seeing the restoration of the apostolic ministry.

God desires His church to be as it was at the beginning. Looking again at the prophetic ministry within the church, we see its vital importance in bringing about the transition. The prophetic utterances that are given, help activate and release the plans and purposes of God within the local church.

Isaiah 40:3 prophetic word said that *one would come crying in the wilderness,* to prepare for a creative word that would change everything in every place. The prophetic word is a creative word. It brings forth life and helps trigger things inside the believer that stirs them and motivates them to fulfill their destiny. Once things are called forth and brought up into the hearts and minds of the believers, then the apostolic and prophetic team can release them and train them into ministry. Prophetic utterances are instrumental in establishing God's will, not just in the local church, but also upon the Earth.

There are many things that cannot be released, unless God speaks them through the prophets. The prophetic word releases, activates, encourages, comforts, and brings confirmation to the hearts and lives of the church. Prophecy given through and by the office of the prophet is a building gift. I cannot at this juncture, overemphasize the importance of prophecy within our churches. Prophecy is such a vital part and according to **1 Corinthians 14:12**, we are to excel and to do extremely well and be proficient in our prophetic word.

Our prophetic words are not to be mediocre; they are not to be given to stroke our soul for the right direction, but they are to be given for the purpose of instruction and edifying the believer in their walk with Christ. This is why it is critical in this hour, that as prophetic and apostolic churches are being birthed, that the apostolic church has, in its midst; a strong prophet who can judge words that are given. It is also important that those learning how to prophesy and not hold back, but it is also an equally important that the prophet, when bringing correction to a prophetic word given, handles the situation in a proper manner for we must speak the truth in love always.

Equipping the Saints for The Church in Transition

The chief and primary role of the Prophet is not just to prophesy, it is to teach everyone how to hear the voice of God for themselves. Jesus said in John 10, *my sheep know my voice*. We want everyone to be trained effectively in hearing the voice of the Lord and distinguishing between the voices of the enemy, their flesh and hearing the voice of the Lord.

There is a huge difference in setting forth the framework of the role of the Prophet in comparison to those in the local church that just prophesy.

What I mean is this, normal prophecy, as we've stated earlier, brings edification, exhorts and comforts as we see this gift working in **1 Corinthians 14:1-5**, but the role of the Prophet is to bring more revelation. The prophets words carry correction, warning, judgment, new direction, and all kinds of things that are different from that of just operating in the gift of prophecy. Prophets are sometimes free- spirited people that choose to come into churches and deliver a message or a word from the Lord, but I feel and sense strongly, that this is the hour when prophets will help build the local church along with the Apostolic.

For the ministry of the Apostolic and Prophetic, when linked together, is a building gift, to build people and to make people mature in Christ that they might do and carry the work of the ministry. Some say that it takes between 10 and 15 years to make a Prophet depending on the access that the prophet has to a good teacher, role model or mentor. I don't know if that is true or not, but I sense that it takes years to develop the character of Christ in most believers. In that period, prophets need to understand that they have a role in the church and that they are not so free- spirited that they are not accountable to local leadership, the local regions, and in local houses of God.

I might also add, that the prophet who prophesies and uses his gift correctly, should be judged by other prophets and prophetic people, because the spirit of the prophet is subject to the prophet. There are too many blessing prophets in our country today, people that are going around giving easy good words, but are not really building the body of Christ. This brings a grave injustice to the body of Christ and those who are trying to build up the body. Prophets build in tough times, they build, and they help set the course for the new church what God is trying to develop in this age and in this time.

As we look at Apostles, they are father figures, whose responsibility it is to develop and produce leadership. They are called wise master builders, who lay the correct spiritual foundations. They will ensure that a church is built upon Jesus Christ, as we see in **1 Corinthians 3:9-16**; the church is built upon the apostles and prophets relating to Jesus as the Chief Cornerstone. I sincerely believe, that in this hour, the Lord has taken His church and is continuing to take His true church into a time of what I call the disassembling season. This is where He will disassemble all forms of religion, all old ways of doing things, and through the apostles and prophet lays new foundations. He does not lay the new foundation upon the old foundation, but I believe that he must utterly destroy and reconstruct leadership, that they might lay proper foundations that bring a dynamic corporate life into the church, that simply wouldn't exist without radical change.

As the church grows, it is the job of the apostles is to set in place, leadership that will represent the oversight to the local body, quality people who are required to carry forth the vision and the atmosphere that the apostles leave in the church. Apostles provide an atmosphere that will help the leaders who carry on the work, when the local apostle is not available, to carry on the anointing and the presence of God that is left there. So, you might say that apostles are facilitators, they try to keep everybody together.

Apostolic Transition and Order

The Apostolic Ministry is given to the church as a master builder to help the habitation of God. The apostolic is devoted to the result of the full maturity of the church. The apostolic and the prophetic anointing rested upon Christ Bible Discipleship Worship Center, it is a corporate anointing to all who receive this calling (**Ephesians 2:9, 22**). The apostolic and prophetic grace is given to every member to explain the kingdom. It is to every member to receive the ability of God to build and equip others and to esteem them greater than ourselves (**2 Corinthians 6:10; 8:9 Philippians 2:3-6**).

The second anointing is your personal calling which is your individual assignment that you must walk out your purpose in the earth whether you are a deacon, elder or usher. The hand of God is sovereign upon this house to conform everyone into the image of His dear son. Even your weakness and strength were already calculated from the foundation of the earth and to carry this ministry to its destiny.

Hebrews 4:7 says, He again fixes a certain day today, *if you hear His voice, don't harden you heart.* But **Deuteronomy 4:29** states, *but if from thence thou shalt seek the Lord your God, thou shalt find him, if thou seek Him with all thy heart and with all thy soul.*

Apostolic order in prophecy, **Malachi 4:5, 6** *Behold, I will send you Elijah the prophet before the coming of the great and dreadful day of the LORD: And he shall turn the heart of the fathers to the children, and the heart of the children to their fathers, lest I come and smite the earth with a curse.*

The Apostle Paul picked up on this in **1 Corinthians 4:14, 15:** *I write not these things to shame you, but as my beloved sons I warn you. For though ye have ten thousand instructors in Christ, yet have ye not many fathers: for in Christ Jesus I have begotten you through the gospel.* The apostolic order and function will be laid out later in this book. The apostolic order is as in the prophetic words of **Jeremiah 23:4**, *And I will set up shepherds over them which shall feed them: and they shall fear no more, nor be dismayed, neither shall they be lacking, saith the LORD.*

In **Exodus 18:3**, Moses was set to judge the people all day until Jethro gave wiser counsel and in **Numbers 11:16**, God told him to choose the seventy elders to help carry out the burden.

It must be God's order in **2 Timothy 2:5** *And if a man also strive for masteries, yet is he not crowned, except he strive lawfully.*

2 Timothy 2:20 *But in a great house there are not only vessels of gold and of silver, but also of wood and of earth; and some to honour, and some to dishonour.*

Malachi 3:3 *And he shall sit as a refiner and purifier of silver: and he shall purify the sons of Levi, and purge them as gold and silver, they may offer unto the LORD and offering in righteousness.*

7

1 Corinthians 9:24 *Know ye not that ye may obtain. And every man that striveth for the mastery is temperate in all things. Now they do it to obtain a corruptible crown; but we an incorruptible. I therefore so run, not as uncertainly; so, fight I, not as one that beateth the air: but I keep under my body, and bring it into subjection: lest that by any means, when I have preached to others, I myself should be a castaway.*

Apostolic Team Ministry will be used to release greater supplies from His storehouse for the last days ministry. New teams and new streams are emerging every day.

1. It will be apostolic, authentic, and abandoned Christianity.
2. It will be telescopic; with prophets looking down the telescope of time and evangelists telling the good news.
3. It will be microscopic with pastors and administrates caring of the house. Restoring the ATM (Apostolic Team Ministry) is building spiritual houses,

1 Corinthians 3:10-11 *According to the grace of God which is given unto me, as a wise master builder, I have laid the foundation and another buildeth thereon. But let every man take heed how he buildeth thereupon. For other foundation can no man lay than that is laid, which is Jesus Christ.*

1 Peter 2:5 *Ye also, as lively stones, are built up a spiritual house, a holy priesthood, to offer up spiritual sacrifices, acceptable to God by Jesus Christ.* The ATM must be restored. Because we the children of Adam want to become great, he became small, (Jesus). Because we will not stoop, he humbles himself, because we want to rule, He came to serve.

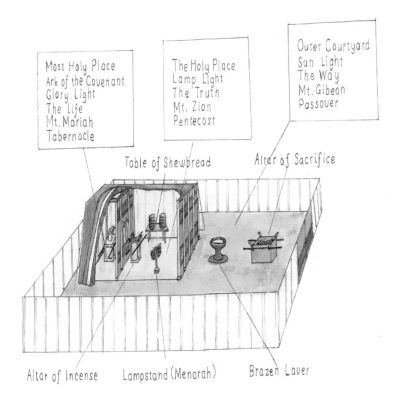

Most Holy Place
Ark of the Covenant
Glory Light
The Life
Mt. Mariah
Tabernacle

The Holy Place
Lamp Light
The Truth
Mt. Zion
Pentecost

Outer Courtyard
Sun Light
The Way
Mt. Gibeon
Passover

Table of Shewbread

Altar of Sacrifice

Altar of Incense

Lampstand (Menorah)

Brazen Laver

9

Chapter 2
Tabernacle of Moses

In the beginning, God and man were in perfect union. They walked together in the cool of the day. God made them in His image. It was His intent to be relational with us. Then Man sinned, and the breach was made. Don't think this took God by surprise, for He states, "Remember the former things of old, for I am God, and there is no other; there is none like ME. declaring the end from the beginning, and from ancient times, things that are not yet done." (**Isaiah 46:9 & 10**)

The divine purpose of God's heart for the building of The Tabernacle is found in **Exodus 25:8**: "Let them make me a sanctuary, that I may dwell among them," God desires to dwell among His people. God gave Moses a pattern or way of approaching God's presence.

THE PATTERN Exodus 26 & 27 (diagram pg. 9)

The Tabernacle of Moses was simply a portable tent with various curtains and coverings over a wooden structure. It had three places to it: **The Outer Court, The Holy Place**, and **The Holiest of All**, or **The Holiest of Holies**.

The Outer Court

THE ALTAR OF SACRIFICE is the first thing you would see as you enter through the gate into the outer court. It was made of acacia wood and overlaid with brass, which came from the looking glasses (mirror) gathered from the women of Egypt. The altar was where the priests sacrificed the animals to atone for the sins of the people. This was a place of death, blood, and atonement. (This represents Christ's sacrifice of His life for us.)

THE BRAZEN LAVER would be the next thing the priest would approach. It was made of highly polished, reflective metal, filled with water that came from the ROCK that Moses struck. The priest would wash the blood from his hands while seeing his reflection through the blood of sacrifice and the water. (This represents water baptism.)

The Altar of Sacrifice and **The Brazen Laver are both** in **The Outer Court** and are illuminated by SUNLIGHT. **The Outer Court** represents Mount Gibeon and The Feast of Passover, which will be discussed more in depth later.

The Holy Place

The priest would then enter **The Holy Place** by walking between five pillars, which refers to the Five-Fold Ministry spoken of in Ephesians 4:11. The pillars also represent grace. They would walk through a curtain that was being held up by the pillars and enter into **The Holy Place**. The curtain was made from blue, purple, and scarlet thread, representing heaven, majesty, and blood.

THE GOLDEN LAMPSTAND would be the first thing the priest would see as they came through the curtain into **The Holy Place. The Golden Lampstand** was made from one single piece of pure gold, which was beaten to form one main shaft with six branches, making seven branches in total, each with a lamp on its end. The branches had a total of 66 ornamentations on them. The ornamentations represent the 66 books of the Bible! The lamps were filled daily with oil and burnt continually before the Lord.

THE TABLE OF SHEWBREAD was across the room from the lampstand. The table was wood overlaid with gold. On top of the table were 12 loaves of bread, which was for the priests. It was called presence bread.

THE ALTAR OF INCENSE is the third article of furniture and was made of wood overlaid with gold. Incense of fragrant spices and shellfish burned here continually before the Lord. Its fragrance filled the sanctuary and symbolized prayer, worship, and intercession. It is set directly before the veil of The Holy of Holies. The veil consisted of the blue, purple, and scarlet thread, as in the other curtain. In this veil we have cherubim embroidered on them in pure gold thread. The Holy Place was illuminated by LAMP LIGHT.

The Holy Place represents Mount Zion and The Feast of Pentecost, to be discussed later.

The Holy of Holies

THE ARK OF THE COVENANT is the only piece of furniture in **The Holy of Holies**. It was made of acacia wood overlaid with gold. On either end of **The Ark** was a figure of a cherubim. Inside **The Ark** was **The Rod of Aaron, The Tablets of the 10 Commandments**, and the **Jar of Manna**, where GOD dwelt. His presence could be seen from the camp and surrounding area as a Cloud by day and a Fire by night in the sky above **The Holy of Holies**.

The Holiest of Holies was illuminated by GLORY light!

It's represented by Mount Moriah and The Feast of Tabernacles, which will be discussed later.

It was in the **Holiest of Holies** or **The Holiest of All** that God's very presence and Shekinah Glory dwelt. It's where God communicated with man, dwelling in the midst of His people, Israel, just as even now, the Presence of Christ dwells in the midst of His people. God has dwelt with men, amongst men, and finally, in men. We become the Tabernacle!

Chapter 3
The Mountains of God

Proverbs 22:20-*Have not I written to thee excellent things in counsels and knowledge. That I might make thee know the certainty of the words of truth: That thou mightiest answer the words of truth to them that send unto thee?*

This truth on the Mountains of God, are seen in the three feasts of Israel Passover, Pentecost, and Tabernacle.

John 14:6-*Jesus said it this way, I Am the way, (Passover), The truth (Pentecost), and the Life (Tabernacle).*

Jesus Christ is the only way into the presence of the mountains of God. In **John 14:6** Jesus declare that *no man cometh unto the Father but by Me* (Passover). **John 16:13** Jesus said, *How be it when He, the Spirit of Truth is come, He will guide you into all truth (Pentecost), for He shall not speak of Himself; But whatsoever He shall hear; that shall He speak: And He will shew you things to come.*

Revelation 21:3-*And I heard a great voice out of heaven saying, Behold the Tabernacle of God is with men and He will dwell with them and be their God (Tabernacle).*

The first place the Ark of covenant was found, was the **"Tent of Meeting,"** that God had commanded Moses to build. God wanted to dwell among His PEOPLE - *The Israelites*. He wanted to have fellowship to be able to communicate with them. This tent of meeting was constructed according to a set pattern by God, not by Moses. This pattern was the only way a sinful people could approach a Holy God.

Hebrews 9:22,23 *And almost all things are by law purged with blood; and without shedding of blood is no remission of sin. It was therefore necessary that the patterns of things in the heavens should be purified with these; but the heavenly things themselves with better sacrifices than these (Jesus Christ) the way.*

In the days of King Solomon, the Tabernacle was on Mt. Gibeon, but the Ark of the Covenant was on Mt. Zion according to **2 Chronicles 1:1-4** - *And Solomon the son of King David was strengthened in his kingdom, and the LORD his God was with him, and magnified him exceedingly. Then Solomon spake unto all Israel to the captains of thousands and of hundreds and to the judges and to every governor in all Israel, the chief of the fathers. So, Solomon and all the congregation with him, went to the high place that was at Gibeon; For there was the Tabernacle of the congregation of God, which Moses the servant of the LORD had made in the wilderness. But the Ark of Covenant of God had King David brought up from Kir-jath-jearim to the place which David had prepared for it; For he had pitched a tent for it at Jerusalem (on Mt. Zion).*

Pentecost the truth: God living in the mist of His people. **Colossians 1:27**- *To make known among the Gentiles the glorious riches of this mystery, which is Christ in you the hope of glory.*

But King Solomon did not go to Mt. Zion first for the Ark of Covenant (or the Presence of God) - **2 Chronicles 1:5** said, *Moreover the brazen alter that Bezaleel the son of Uri, the son Hur, had made, he put before the Tabernacle of the LORD; And Solomon and the congregation SOUGHT unto it. and Solomon went up thither to the BRAZEN ALTAR before the LORD, which was at the Tabernacle of the congregation and offered a thousand burnt offerings upon it. In that night God appear unto Solomon, and said unto him, ASK what I shall I give thee.*

How many would like to have that blank check? All because Solomon SOUGHT for the BRAZEN ALTAR, and the condition for the heart of the people of Israel, to be right with GOD, after many days of sacrifices. So, Solomon asked for wisdom and knowledge to lead God's people.

So, in the King Solomon season; because this was in Solomon's heart; God granted unto him, in verse twelve, wisdom and knowledge; and God gave him riches, wealth, and honor such as none of the kings before him.

If you would like to have Mt. Zion and Mt. Moriah, you must visit Mt. Gibeon (Passover) were the sin was dealt with before the Pentecost experience on Mt. Zion, and the Shekinah Glory on Mt. Moriah (Tabernacle). The pattern is clear, Jesus Christ is the Passover LAMB, without Him being your LORD and king; you will not experience Pentecost or Shekinah Glory.

Back to the King Solomon season; here is the promise. it the season of wisdom, it the season of knowledge, it the season of riches, it the season of wealth, and it the season of honor. These five grace points, brings us into a new season and (Extravagant) life in Christ Jesus.

What the Apostle Paul said in **Ephesians 4:13** - *Till we all come in the unity of the faith and of the knowledge of the Son of God, unto a perfect man, unto the measure of the stature of the fullness of Christ: That we henceforth be no more children, tossed to and fro and carried about with every wind of doctrine by the sleight of men and cunning craftiness, whereby they lie wait to deceive.*

These mountains of God's Grace points, or bigger than any secular mountains in the world. Here they are: **Religion, Family, Education, Government, Media, Arts & Entertainment, and Business**.

The word of the LORD to these mountains of the world.

Zechariah 4:6,7 - *The angel of the LORD answered and spake unto me, saying, this is the word of the LORD unto Zerubbabel saying, not by might, nor by power, but by My Spirit, saith the LORD of Hosts. Who art thou shalt O great mountain? Before Zerubbabel thou shalt become a plain: and he shall bring forth the headstone thereof with shouting, crying, Grace, Grace unto it.* The mountains of God's grace are bigger and greater than any other mountain in the world. Mt. Gibeon (Passover), Mt. Zion (Pentecost), and Mt. Moriah (Tabernacle) are bigger than any mountain. We find in **Ezekiel 37**, a valley of very dry bones. In verse ten it says, *So I prophesied as he commanded me, and the breath came into them, and they lived, and stood up upon their feet an exceeding great army. Then he said unto me, Son of man, these bones are the whole house of Israel: Behold they say, our bones are dried and our hope is lost: we are cut off for our parts.*

We as the body of Christ can no longer be divided on the mountains of God's Grace.

If you are at Mt. Gibeon (Passover) preaching Jesus Christ is the only way to the Father, you have **John 3:16** AND CONFESS ROMANS **10:9**, GREAT but there is more. Do not crucify your brother because he has not received Mt. Zion (Pentecost) or baptized with the Holy Spirit, according to **Acts 2:1-4** - *and when the days of Pentecost was fully come, they were all with one accord in one place. And suddenly there came a sound from heaven as of a rushing mighty wind, and it filled all the house where they were sitting. And there appeared into them clover tongues like as of fire, and it set upon each of them. And they were all filled with the Holy Ghost and began to speak with other tongues as the Spirit gave them utterance.*

Don't crucify your brother because he has not received the baptism of the Holy Ghost. You that have been baptized in the Holy Spirit, don't stop there, look to Mt. Moriah (Tabernacle) for the Shekinah Glory experience.

2 Chronicles 7:1-3;12 - *Now when Solomon had made an end of praying, the fire came down from heaven and consumed the burnt offering and the sacrifices; and the Glory of the LORD filled the house. And the priests could not enter into the house of the LORD, because the glory of the LORD had filled the LORD'S house. And when all the children of Israel saw how the fire came down and the glory of the LORD upon the house, they bowed themselves with their faces to the ground upon the pavement and worshipped and praised the LORD, saying, For He is good; For His mercy endureth forever.*

They that seek after the LORD after having a Mt. Zion (Pentecost) experience:

1. Mt. Moriah, Shekinah Glory
2. Extravagant Worship
3. Extravagant Praises

For King Solomon SOUGHT for the brazen altar first. Before going after Mt. Zion and Mt. Moriah, you must deal with the issue of the heart first.

At the dedication of the Temple in **2 Chronicles 7:9**, it says, *that and in the eighth day, they made a solemn assembly: For they kept the dedication of the alter seven days, and the feast seven days.*

God's presence shows up when people are hungry for God and willing to make the sacrifice to have more. When God Grace you to do more, then do more.

Philippians 2:13 - *For it is God which worketh in you both to will and to do of His good pleasure. Even this the mystery which hath been hid from ages and from generations, but now is made manifest to His saints. To whom God would make know what is the riches of the glory of this mystery among the Gentiles; Which is Christ in you, the hope of Glory:*

God said in **Ezekiel 37:22**, *And I will make them one nation in the land upon the mountains of Israel: and one king shall be king over them all: and they shall be no more two nations, neither shall they be divided into two kingdoms any more at all.*

Here we see that in the mountains of God, Mt. Gibeon, (Passover) Mt. Zion (Pentecost) Mt. Moriah (Tabernacle) God people become one nation and one king shall be there King (Jesus Christ), and there they shall never be divided any more.

Ezekiel 37:26 & 27 says, *Moreover I will make a covenant of peace with them; It shall be an everlasting covenant with them. And I will place them, and* *multiply them and will set my sanctuary in the midst of them for evermore. My tabernacle also shall be with them: Yea, I will be their God and they shall be my people. And the heathen shall know that I the LORD do sanctify Israel, when my sanctuary shall be in the midst of them for evermore.*

The Apostle John, in **Revelation 21:3** said, *And I heard a great voice out of heaven saying, behold ,the tabernacle of God is with men, and He will dwell with them, and they shall be His people, and God Himself shall be with them and be their God.*

The prophet Isaiah, in **Isaiah 65:8** prophecies about the mountains of God, *Thus saith the LORD, as the new wine is found in the cluster, and one saith destroy it not: for a blessing is in it: so will I do for my servants sakes, that I may not destroy them all. And I will bring forth a seed out of Jacob and out of Judah an inheritor of my mountains: and mine elect shall inherit it, and my servants shall dwell there. Amen and Amen.*

The Seven Mountains of Influence, or seven heads, are seven areas which the movement believes controls society and which they seek to control are Religions, Family, Education, Government, Media, Arts & Entertainment, and Business. In the Bible by the prophet Isaiah, a prophecy in **Isaiah 2:2**, says, Now it shall come to pass in the latter days that the mountains of the LORD'S house shall be established on the top of the seven mountains of influence. We, as the five-fold ministry, are empowered by the grace of God to occupy the seven mountains of influence, to transition the mind of the people to trust God of Israel. Transition is the act of making a change from one set of circumstances to another. Some kingdom teaches believe that by fulfilling the Seven Mountains mandate, they can bring about the end times.

Food for Thought

Revelation 17:3 So he carried me away in the spirit into the wilderness: and I saw a woman sit upon a scarlet coloured beast, full of names of blasphemy, having seven heads and ten horns. **4** And the woman was arrayed in purple and scarlet colour, and decked with gold and precious stones and pearls, having a golden cup in her hand full of abominations and filthiness of her fornication: **5** And upon her forehead *was* a name written, MYSTERY, BABYLON THE GREAT, THE MOTHER OF HARLOTS AND ABOMINATIONS OF THE EARTH. **6** And I saw the woman drunken with the blood of the saints, and with the blood of the martyrs of Jesus: and when I saw her, I wondered with great admiration. **7** And the angel said unto me, Wherefore didst thou marvel? I will tell thee the mystery of the woman, and of the beast that carrieth her, which hath the seven heads and ten horns. **8** The beast that thou sawest was, and is not; and shall ascend out of the bottomless pit, and go into perdition: and they that dwell on the earth shall wonder, whose names were not written in the book of life from the foundation of the world, when they behold the beast that was, and is not, and yet is. **9** And here *is* the mind which hath wisdom. The seven heads are seven mountains, on which the woman sitteth. **10** And there are seven kings: five are fallen, and one is, *and* the other is not yet come; and when he cometh, he must continue a short space. **11** And the beast that was, and is not, even he is the eighth, and is of the seven, and goeth into perdition. **12** And the ten horns which thou sawest are ten kings, which have received no kingdom as yet; but receive power as kings one hour with the beast. **13** These have one mind, and shall give their power and strength unto the beast. **14** These shall make war with the Lamb, and the Lamb shall overcome them: for he is Lord of lords, and King of kings: and they that are with him **are** called, and chosen, and faithful. **15** And he saith unto me, The waters which thou sawest, where the whore sitteth, are peoples, and multitudes, and nations, and tongues. **16** And the ten horns which thou sawest upon the beast, these shall hate the whore, and shall make her desolate and naked, and shall eat her flesh, and burn her with fire. **17** For God hath put in their hearts to fulfil his will, and to agree, and give their kingdom unto the beast, until the words of God shall be fulfilled. **18** And the woman which thou sawest is that great city, which reigneth over the kings of the earth.

Chapter 4

Show Us The Pattern

(Excerpts by: Prophet Pat Sparrow)

<u>Traditional Church:</u> *is need based and reactionary*

<u>Apostolic Church:</u> *is visionary and intentional.*

Jesus said *the poor you will have with you always.* Many times, in pastoral ministry, because of the lack of resources and personnel we as Pastors spend much of our time reacting to personal needs. Reacting because this person needs this or that; so the life of the church and the purposes of the pastoral office; are all about reacting to needs.

The church I was at for nine years; we spent just two days of strategic planning. The rest of the time was pretty much reactionary, with very little vision counseling, very little intentional ministry of expanding outward of what God is saying; but that is being changed under Apostolic Administration because Apostles are very vision based and intentional in their gifts.

<u>Traditional Church:</u> short in structural worship vs. spontaneous and Spirit led worship.

That is a big change that has come to the church. We have a somewhat structured Sunday morning service where we sing maybe five songs, because we know that time is different, but the key is that you make room for the Spirit of God to move.

Traditional Church: A mindset of just waiting for Jesus to return.

Apostolic Church: A mindset of we have a destiny to fulfill here and in eternity.

> **Note:** The book *Purpose Driven Life* sold over 22 million copies. There is something that God has put in the heart of people that there is something to fulfill on this side of eternity; whether they are saved or unsaved.

Traditional Church: Believing people will come to church and get saved.

Apostolic Church: The apostolic mindset is we are sent into all the world to preach and demonstrate the power of the Gospel. We do not wait for them, but begin to prayer walk and strategize over cities and begin to understand where strongholds are and portals of darkness, and begin to bind up and loose and intentionally do warfare that bands of wickedness are broken and people begin to receive the Gospel.

It is intentional and strategic.

Traditional Church: puts emphasis on the facility. (building)

Apostolic Church: puts emphasis on function. The idea of what we can do in a community to gather saints. There is great creativity being released in that area.

Traditional Church: is a place for people to attend. Apostolic Church: is a place for people to connect. Traditional Church:

A. More people
B. Commitment to attendance
C. Emphasis on loyalty to the Pastor, local church and denomination
D. Have events to attract people
E. Puts emphasis on the importance of personal performance

Apostolic Church:

A. Growing people
B. Commitment to relationships (including leadership)
C. Emphasis on loyalty to Christ, to His Kingdom while serving the local church but loyalty is to the King and the Kingdom being expressed through serving the local church.
D. Have events to build people
E. Puts emphasis on the importance of training others.

We must create a church culture that celebrates risks rather than great performances. We applaud because the people took the chance to move forward in the things of God not based on how good they perform. This is a shift of mindset that must come.

Traditional Church:

A. Series of unconnected events
B. Proper homiletic or (proper preaching) presentation
C. We teach parents and entertain the children
D. Building the individual church is the whole emphasis
E. We have charitable giving

Apostolic Church:

A. Strategic systems and teaching
B. Anointed messages and anointed messengers. In our value system we value the anointing. It becomes the standard.
C. We teach and train both parents and children.
D. Building the kingdom. We understand that we are a part of the worldwide church.
E. Purposeful giving. Supporting a mandate to go throughout the earth, because the tithe will not do what God has in mind for the planet.

Chapter 5
The Testimony of John Crowder

In the 1990s during a Christian TV program, I received a phone call for prayer. This Christian woman, Miss Crowder calls in for prayer. My wife, Lillie and I went to her home to pray for her. As we prayed, she asked me to mentor her son. I was thinking about a young man, but find out, He was the same age as me. His name was John, and John had many problems; the world had a big hold on him.

So, I started work with him. I didn't know that this journey would cost me so much of my time, patience, and faith. The community knew that I was a mentor to him. Every time he got in trouble, they would call me. Sometimes late at night, I would have to go and get him out of many situations.

One time, I got a phone call from McCain Correctional Hospital, telling me that John was in there with gangrene. He was in a coma and they weren't expecting him to leave the hospital alive. So, I called his mother to go and visit John that Saturday; Me, his mother, and sister went to see him, at McCain Hospital. When we got there, I said to his mother, "Let me go in first." I did not know what to expect, so as I walked down the hallway, a man stepped out from a room and said to me, "Don't worry, he is being taken down the *Roman's Road*, and he stepped back into the room. When I got to where John was, he was in a coma, with his feet bandaged up.

On my way back to his mother, the room that the man stepped out of, was open. To my surprise, it was a closet. My faith increased, for I believe that God sent an angel to encourage me. His mother and I went into the room. She began to pray and we came into agreement, that God would raise John up. I called out to John, to praise his way out of this coma; as we held on to the horn of the altar, calling out in the name of Jesus Christ; nothing happens.

We went home and that Sunday morning, as I entered my office at church, the phone rang. I answered and the voice said,

"This is John."

I said, "Who?"

"This is John. I heard you and mother praying for me. When you said praise your way out of this, I began to sing the song of Zion, and I woke up praising God. Fear came over the attendant, and they ran out of the room."

Many miracles happened with John. One time, he was in a boarding house and they call me to come and get him. He was very sick. I went to pick him up at 3'o clock in the morning and found him in a fetal position in the corner, out of his head, and he could not walk; I had to carry him to my truck. I headed to the hospital and did not tell anyone where I was taking him. I decided not to stop at the first hospital, but went on to the next hospital in Charlotte, which was farther away. When I pulled up to the emergency room, two women in white were waiting on us. They said to me, "Pastor Allen, go home and rest we got him."

Two things to note here: one, no one knew where I was going, and two, how did they know my name? Again, God sent his angels to help me out; John got out of the hospital a week later. He came to church and testified about how God had saved him.

That Monday, he got on a bicycle and rode around the city of Monroe but his heart was too weak; He died in hospice that Tuesday. I was asked to do his home going service. As I was walking in front of the procession, I heard God said, "Now I can trust you with my sons." I started thinking, that I was there for John, but all the time, John was also there for me. How I handled John would determine what God would release to me. This is how I was entrusted with the Apostolic Ministry.

Chapter 6
Kingdom Order

Our purpose is the Glory of the Lord touching the earth.

Moses

Set man - Father - 1 Corinthians 4:14, 17

A. Need to desire sons and following a father;
    Galatians 4:5, 6

B. Establishing the church in present day truth;
    II Peter 1:12, 14

C. Establishing Generational Order-
    Galatians 3:14; Genesis 25:58

D. Assembling the Body – **Ephesians 4:12, 16**

E. Give body Identity, Purpose, Vision, Inheritance, Blessing

F. Christ the pattern – **Philippians 2:1-30**

Aaron

Elder - Over the Priestly Order - Exodus 40:12, 16

A. The sons of Aaron- **Leviticus 1:7; 3:13**

B. Anointing of Aaron – **Leviticus 7:35**

C. Aaron was an instrument of miracles - **Exodus 7:8, 20**

D. Aaron was Moses' mouthpiece to the congregation **Exodus 16:9, 10**

E. Aaron was to lay up the testimony of the Lord for the next generation - **Exodus 16:33, 34**

F. Aaron was honor with fellowship with Moses - **Exodus 18:12**

Joshua

Son - Moses' Ministry - Exodus 24:13

A. Generational Order

B. Son fights all fleshy issues - **Exodus 17:9**

C. A son stays close to the fathers' heart - **Exodus 33:11, 17**

D. A son guards his father – **Number 11:28, 29**

E. A son receives inheritance - **Number 27:18, 22**

Elders

70 - Carriers of The Vision - Exodus 24: 1, 9,14; They saw God

A. Faithful men – **Numbers 11:25**

B. Help build proper order - D**euteronomy 27:1, 3 Deuteronomy 31:9**

C. Speak into the next generations - **Deuteronomy 32:7**

D. Able to hold the people to the vision- **Judges 2:7, 8**

E. Has the ability to service the son in ministry when transition takes place - **Joshua 7:6, Joshua 23:2,4**

Chapter 7
What Is The House Really Like?

Apostolic Houses

Without proper identification, you cannot steer the ship.

Ephesians 4:16

A. Vision and strategy, government, rank, and order.

B. Prophetic expression, sound preaching and teaching, allowing for exploration that moves into the realm of revelation.

C. Stable families, where family centered values are taught and practiced.

D. Prayer. A house filled with intercessors, with much teaching about the purpose of prayer.

E. Prosperity and blessing, where there are signs of prosperity by what is taught.

F. Bold faith, where faith takes preeminence and faith goes into new territory and new ground.

G. Healing, miracles, deliverance, missions, praise, and worship.

H. Social care, where the needs of people are being met in practical ways.

I. Gifts of the spirit and the spiritual gifts.

J.   Leadership training, discipleship, mentoring, and developing children and youth for the future.

K.   Business entities, where entrepreneurs provide financially.

L.   Technology; where technological pursuits are insisted upon.

People are misidentified all the time. We must properly identify the offices and giftings of leaders and people in the congregation for the ministry to be most effective.

Chapter 8
Church Leadership

LOCAL

Along with the five-fold ministry. God has also ordained leadership ministries which are basically to work with the local body of believers. These local ministries give oversight to the Lord's work in both the spiritual and physical realms.

Persons involved in these ministries live and function with the believers on a daily "basis." This availability allows for leading by "example" and creating a vital strengthening and caring ability.

These local ministries are:

Pastors, Elders, Ruling Elders (See Numbers 11:17).

I. ELDERS (Titus 5)

Elders are those who work the closest with the five-fold in keeping watch on the spiritual condition of the body. They are to give spiritual oversight to the body. Their spiritual gifts and abilities may vary, but these men jointly are to be spiritual pillars in the local assembly.

1) They give oversight to the church of God. **(Acts 20:28)**

   a. Oversight implies "a head above" (not to be interpreted as being better than), but able to observe what is happening in any given direction.

    b. Reason for the oversight role is because of grievous wolves and men arising from within to draw away disciples. **(Acts 20:29-30)**

2) They are to feed the church of God. **(Acts 20:28)**

    a. This does not mean that all Elders must be "teachers" or "preachers." It means they are to be responsible for making sure the flock is feed properly. **(1 Timothy 5:17)**

3) They are channels of God's healing to the body. **(James 5:14-15)**

    a. It is important to note, they are to be channels of healing. The person needing healing calls for the Elders and confess sin if any has been committed.

4) They are the instrument by which an individual's calling is confirmed. **(1 Timothy 4:14)**

    a. The word "gift" (charisma) can mean religious qualification.

5) There are to be examples to the body. **(1 Peter 5:3-6)**

    a. "Example" means pattern (Greek "*tupos*"). They are to show forth the will and way of the Lord by their life actions.

Elders are to serve with the right motivations.

1) They are to serve not by compelled of necessity: compulsorily (seeing it restrictive), but willingly. **(1 Peter 5:2)**
2) They are not to serve for monetary gain, but of ready (eager) mind. **(1 Peter 5:2)**
3) They are not to have a "lording" attitude, but one of humility and service. **(1 Peter 5:3)**
4) Their encouragement should stem from the eternal value of their office. **(1 Peter 5:4)**

Prayer moves the arm that moves the world to bring deliverance down to move people. The leader must be able to move God.

There are other terms synonymous with the word "Elder."

1) Elder taken from the Greek, "**presbuterouss**," means "senior" (**Acts 14:23, 1 Timothy 5:17**). Rule-to be over; to preside over-to have to care of.

   a) This is not to be confused with the other meaning it has denoting age. (**1 Timothy 5:1**)

   b) It indicates maturity of spiritual experience.

2) Bishop, taken from the Greek "*episkopos*" means "overseer." (**Acts 20: 26-28; Philippians 1:1, 1 Timothy 3:1**)

   a) This indicates how to function. (**1 Peter 2:5, John 10:16, Zechariah 10:2, 11:16**)

II. DEACONS (Phil. 1:1)

Deacons are those who are responsible to give oversight to the physical needs in the body. They are to be spiritual individuals who free the Elders to give their attention to spiritual matters. (**Acts 6:1-3**)

1. They are to function at the serving tables. (**Acts 6:2**)

   a. Serving tables were places where collections were received and distributions to people were made.

   b. The qualifications for Deacons are found in **Acts 6:3 and 1 Timothy 3:8-12.**

   c. The office of Deacon when used properly provides for a person to obtain a good degree (standing), great boldness in faith (**1 Tim, 3:13**) and great opportunities to be used of the Lord. (**Acts 6:8**)

III. HELPS (1 Corinthians 12:28)

The *"helps"* ministry is a supernatural ministry. This ministry gift is listed along with the others such as miracles and healing. The gift of helps has been set in the Church of God as concrete pillars to "help" hold everything up. God has set in each church a Pastor/Elder team with a vision and responsibility to oversee it. This ministry gift helps the leadership to run the Church effectively and efficiently bring the vision to pass. Without this ministry, your church and leadership would be greatly handicapped, like a hand without fingers. Every one, men, women, and children are called to this supernatural ministry. **(Ephesians 4:15, 16)**

A. Persons involved in this helps ministry, under the Elder's oversight, are responsible for many areas. The following are:

    1. Outreach such as soul-winning efforts; hospital, nursing home and prison visitation.

    2. Prayers of intercession and supplication

    3. Ministries in the church such as: ushering, audio/visuals, hosting, teaching children, and maintenance.

    4. Realms of service to others. **1 Kings 6:7** build the house of the Lord. **1 Kings 10:4,6** the house that takes the breath away.

B. The importance of this ministry cannot be stressed enough. Helpers in the church are of immeasurable value and a vital part of the foundation of all successful churches.

    1. It is God honored ministry.

    a. It will be rewarded. **(Matthew 25:21; Luke 19:17)**

    b. A person involved in this ministry was raised from the dead. **(Acts 9:36-44)**

    c. It is a manifestation of His indwelling presence **(1 John 3:16-18)**

    d. It is something we are all encouraged to do. **(Ecclesiastes 9:10)**

IV. GOVERNMENTS (1 Corinthians 12:28)

A. Those in ministry of administration are ones who can take a given plan of action, organize it, delegate responsibility, and see that it is carried out.

1. Governments, aken from the Greek "kubernesis," means "a steering, pilotage, a guiding."

   a. It has no reference to power to rule, but to persons of extraordinary wisdom, knowledge, and discernment to guide the church in accomplishing its tasks.

   b. In most cases, this would involve ministry to a task rather than a ministry to people

   c. They give continuity to the helps ministry.

V. GOVERNMENT

Earthly authority; those who rule over others to keep society stable and orderly. Only God is the sovereign ruler of all. When human governments exalt themselves above God, they go beyond their legitimate function in society. **(Daniel 5:23)** In Bible times God exercised government through many persons and institutions.

The basic unit of government among the Hebrews was the "fathers house" or primary family **(Genesis 12:1, Numbers 1:4)**. Above this was the clan **(Numbers 36:6)** and then the tribe, governed by a leader who was chosen by representatives from the tribes **(Numbers 1:4-16)**. Over all these units was a central leader. In early days, Moses, or Joshua (and Aaron and his descendants in the religious sphere) served as central leaders among the Israelites. After Joshua's death, numerous local or tribal leaders known as Judges stepped forward to lead. These judges exercised many governmental functions, but no central leadership existed during those days. Only Samuel approached national status as a leader.

The possibility of a king as central leader of the nation was foreseen as early as **Deuteronomy 17:14-20**. The kings governed by using bureaucracies like those of other ancient near Eastern kingdoms. Kings who overstepped the legitimate bounds of "government under God" were often confronted by prophets such as Elijah, Nathan, or Jeremiah (**2 Samuel 12:1-15**).

Isaiah the prophet pointed to the coming Messiah who would be the supreme ruling king and agency of God's government of His people (**Isaiah 9:6-7**).

After the fall of Jerusalem in 587 B.C., the Jews were ruled by foreign powers such as Babylon, Persia, Greece, and Rome. During most of these times, however, the Jews were a measure of self-government. In time the office of High Priest took on political as well as religious dimensions. At most times there was also a group of local Jewish leaders that formed a governing council. In Jesus' day this body was called the Sanhedrin. Made up of both Sadducees and Pharisees, it was presided over by the high priest.

Jesus taught that earthly governments exist by God's will (**John 19:11**) and are legitimate if they do not take over the role reserved for God alone (**Mark 12:13-17**). Romans 13 discusses human government as ordained by God. Revelation 13 on the other hand, discusses it as a degenerate and demonic. Christians live in the tension created by the fact that governments can be good (Romans 13) or evil (Revelation 13). When governments promote good and suppress evil, they fulfil their God given function (**1 Peter 2:11-12**). But if government exalts itself as sovereign over all life, then it has overstepped its bounds and is a handmaid of evil.

Chapter 9
Church Leadership

APOSTOLIC TRANSLOCAL TEAM

God ordained leadership and structure in the church is vital for the growth and effectiveness of the believer. God's Word supplies the plan for proper structure and direction. Yet, it still allows the freedom necessary for the Holy Spirit to move in the church and in the life of every believer.

Then scriptural pattern for leadership is both local and trans local. We will be looking in to trans local leadership (leadership to more than one locality or congregation) in this teaching.

I. REASONS FOR LEADERSHIP IN THE CHURCH:

A. **Ephesians 4:7-16** tells us that God has given ministries of leadership as gifts to the church:

    1. For the equipping of the saints for the work of the ministry

    2. To bring about unity of the faith.

    3. To bring all to the knowledge of the Son of God (an ongoing, personal relationship)

    4. To bring the saints to maturity in Jesus.

B. To maintain order. The church of Jesus Christ is pictured as an army and the saints as soldiers (**II Timothy 2:3**). An army needs to work together as a unit with a common goal. To help accomplish this in the church, God has ordained leadership and structure.

C. As examples in speech, conduct, love, faith and purity (**I Timothy 4:12**). The most effective way to lead or teach is by example. This is true in any area of life, but especially in the church.

D. To serve the body of Christ by providing encouragement and meeting the needs of the saints.

II. QUALIFICATIONS FOR THOSE IN LEADERSHIP:

According to **1 Timothy 3**, one in leadership must be:

1. Blameless: above reproach, above scorn, rebuke, or shame: suffer **1 Timothy 3:7, 2 Corinthians 12:10.**

2. The husband of one wife, temperate, sober, sound mind.

3. Prudent, respectable, good behavior, hospitable.

4. Able to teach (not necessarily from the pulpit).

5. Not addicted to wine or violence.

6. Gentle kind demeanor.

7. Uncontentious must be peaceable, not to take up a guard.

8. Free from the love of money.

9. One who manage his own household well.

10. Not a new convert.

11. Have a good reputation with those outside the church.

B. Leaders are to shepherd the flock, exercising oversight not under compulsion, but voluntarily, not for sordid gain, and not lord it over those in their charge, but be examples to the flock (**1 Peter 5:2, 3).**

C. Leaders must be servants Jesus said, "let him who is great among you become as the youngest, and the leader as the servant (**Luke 22:26 NASB).**

III. WHAT IS THE TRANSLOCAL MINISTRY OF LEADERSHIP ORDAINED BY GOD AND WHAT IS ITS FUNCTION?

It is what is commonly referred to as the five- fold ministry, listed in **Ephesians 4:11**, apostles, prophets, evangelists, pastors, and teachers. Being as it were, the hand of God to minister to the church, let us liken each ministry to a finger of the hand: apostle being the thumb, the prophet being the fore-finger, the evangelist the middle finger, the pastor the ring finger and the teacher the little finger.

1. APOSTLE (the thumb): The apostle is the first ministry gift listed in **1 Corinthians 12:28**. His whole life is devoted to the church and his whole desire is to present the church spotless to the Lord. His work is foundational **(Ephesians 2:20)** and he works as a master builder, as one would work with stones to make a building **(1 Peter 2:5)**. Being the thumb of the hand, he can touch all four of the other ministries and function in each as needed. The word "*apostle*" comes from the Greek word "*apostolos*" meaning "one sent forth." The apostolic anointing is very different from other ministry gifts. Once leaders understand the various functions of their own office, only then can they move and function in their full anointing.

A. Apostles are pioneers

B. Apostles plant churches

C. Apostles reform and bring change

D. Apostles are ordained elders

E. Apostles teach, preach, and set doctrine

F. Apostles release revelation concerning the plans of God for His people (the church)

G. Apostles establish teams

H. Apostles oversee churches

I. Apostles confirm and strengthen local churches

37

J. Apostles bring judgment and conviction

K. Apostles defend the faith

L. Apostles gather

2. PROPHET (the fore-finger): The prophet is also a foundational ministry in the Church **(Ephesians 2:20)**. He, along with the apostles, has the largest vision for the church. The word "*prophet*" comes from the Greek word "*prophetess*" meaning "one who speaks forth; a proclaimed or a divine message.

A. He is a watchman of the church **(Ezekiel 3:17, 33:1-9)**. The prophet acts as a watchman on the wall for sin, blessings, attacks from the enemy or needs in the body.

B. He is the burden-bearer **(Ezekiel 4:4-6)**. Ezekiel was a type of Christ; the New Testament prophet, as a burden-bearer with Christ, seeks to complement what Christ accomplished at Calvary.

C. As the fore-finger of the hand, he sees and points out blessings, sins and needs in the body.

D. He brings forth revelation of the scriptures. **(1 Corinthians 14:30)**

E. He provides direction in ministry, doctrine, and worship. **(Acts 15:32)**

F. He confirms and imparts spiritual gifts and blessings. **(Acts 15:32)**

G. He has the ministry of confirming God's motives and will.

3. EVANGELIST (middle finger): Being the middle finger of the hand, the evangelist is the one with the "longest reach." He has a great burden for the lost. It is important to keep in mind that this ministry was given to the church **(Ephesians 4:11, 12)** to stir us up and teach us to reach the lost. The word "*evangel-ist*" comes from the Greek word "evange-lists" meaning "a messenger of good."

A. He exhorts men to repent, believe and obey the "Gospel." **(2 Timothy 4:2,5)**

B. He extends the gospel message to new areas **(Acts 8:4; 11:19-21)**

C. He has the ministry of stirrings

4. PASTOR (ring finger): The pastor, more so than the four, is more locally oriented. Being the ring finger, he is the one with the strongest "covenant relationship" to the local body of believers. Whereas, the others generally have a larger vision of the church, the pastor is given the vision for the local body, and he will nurture, shepherd, and serve that body to bring that vision to fulfillment.

He encourages the pastoral gift in the local Eldership, and the body to a greater and more effective nurturing. The word "pastor" comes from the Greek word "poimen," meaning "a shepherd; one who tends flocks.

A. He feeds **(1 Peter 5:2-4; John 21:16)**

B. He protects **(Acts 20:28-31; Hebrews 13:17)**

C. He guides **(John 10:3,4)**

D. He is willing to lay down his life for the flock **(John 10:11-13)**

5. TEACHER (little finger): The little finger of the hand is what enables us to grip an object (such as a hammer) strongly. When missing, the greater percentage of our gripping strength is gone. Likewise, the teacher is one who gives us a strong grip on the Word of God. The word *"teacher"* comes from the Greek word *"did-askalos"* meaning "amaster."

A. He builds on the foundation laid by the apostles and prophets to establish the saints **(1 Corinthians 3).**

B. He clarifies the truth in a way that enables us to be obedient to the Word of God.

C. He communicates in a way that motivates one to study the scriptures.

D. He reveals truth in a way that brings unity and stability through understanding **(1 Corinthians 1:10).**

E. He has the ministry of stabilizing andstrengthening.

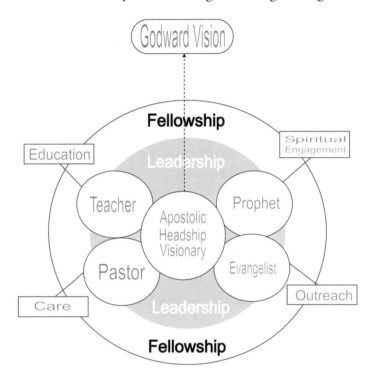

1. **Apostle**-Christ the Sent One
2. **Prophet**-Christ the Word of God, God's, spokesman
3. **Evangelist**-Christ the Good Tiding
4. **Pastor**-Christ our Shepherd
5. **Teacher**-Christ the Revelation of God

IV. PURPOSE OF TRANSLOCAL TEAM LEADERSHIP

A. They are seasoned experienced men in the workings of the Lord, able to assist the local leadership in establishing the local ministry: Because of personal experience **(1 John 1:1- 4)**. Because of a call of the Holy Spirit acknowledged by the local leadership **(Acts 13:1-3)**. Because of personal ministry in given locations with results **(Acts 14:19- 23)**.

B. They can instruct the local leadership and assembly: In the ways of the Lord **(Acts 15:6-11; 13-20)**, In matters of church relationships **(1 Corinthians 3)**, holiness **(1 Corinthians 5:10)**, and ministry **(1 Corinthians 11-14)**. Through clarification of doctrine **(1 Corinthians 15)** and warnings against departing from it **(Galatians 1:6-9)**.

C. They can resolve conflicts and errors with God given authority **(2 Corinthians 12:19, 13:10)**. Although the church down through the ages has altered or rejected the fivefold ministry, it still stands as the Lord's pattern for His church. Along with the renewal of the church through the outpouring of the Holy Spirit, is a stirring back to the Lord's pattern of the fivefold. Acceptance of His pattern will; strengthen the ministry of believers and the local church, propel the work of the Lord forward in a great power, and again makes the church that force "that the gates of hell cannot prevail against." A proper understanding of the trans local ministry and embracing of it is vital.

Chapter 10

Responsibilities of The Flock Towards Leadership

So then, "as you have received Christ Jesus the Lord, walk in Him, having been rooted and being built up in Him, and being confirmed in the faith just as you were taught" **(Colossians 2:6-7).**

The hope and prayer of this ministry is that, having come this far, each of you has allowed your life to be deeply rooted and established in Christ and him in you. The absence of this accomplished work in our lives only spells unnecessary trouble down the road.

Our objective and goal are to grow up to mature, both individually and collectively as we make up a small part of the Body of Christ. Growth and development are accomplished through various means: the Word, the Spirit, the ministry, right relationship to others in the body. But whether alone or together, God requires faithfulness to the added responsibilities which go hand- in-hand with maturity.

As we have entered covenant relationship to God, we find ourselves committed not only to Him, but also to all those who make up His body. In such a relationship, the depth of our maturity is tested, and we stand accountable to God in our faithfulness to such.

A. To the Pastors:

    a. Support in prayer **(Romans 15:30)**

    b. Honor, respect, appreciate and love **(Philippians 2:29; 1 Thessalonians 5:12- 13)**

    c. Monetary support **(1 Corinthains 9:6-14; Galatians 6:6; 1 Timothy 5:17-18)**

    d. Cooperate in fulfilling God's directions conveyed through them **(Hebrews 13:17)**

B. To fellow members of the Body **(1 Corinthians 12:25)**

    a. Ministering spiritual abilities **(1 Corinthians 14:26; 1 Peter 4:10)**

    b. Prayer and intercession **(2 Corinthains 1:11; Ephesians 6:18)**

    c. Love **(Colossians 2:2, Hebrews 13:1; 1 Peter 2:17)**

    d. Comfort **(1 Corinthians 1:4; 1 Thessalonians 4:18)**

    e. Hospitality **(Romans 12:13; Hebrews 13:2; 1 Peter 4:9)**

    f. Time and strength **(Proverbs 3:27; Galatians 6:10)**

    g. Money and possessions **(Romans 12:13; 1 John 3:17)**

Chapter 11
The Team Presbytery at Work

God has purposed for the church, the Body of Christ, to be alive and vibrant witnesses until he removes it from this world. As it progresses from generation to generation and culture to culture, it at times faces circumstances, beliefs and ministry needs that may not be specifically spoken to from the Word. Mention is made in the scripture of the presbytery which can be part of God's provision for the church in facing the above situations.

I. WHAT IS THE PRESBYTERY?

A. The actual word is mentioned in the Bible. It comes from the Greek word "presbuterion" and is translated "elders" **(Luke 22:66; Acts 22:5)** and "presbytery" **(1 Timothy 4:14)**. One author has commented that this word was not a new one used of church elders, but was a familiar official title used in trade unions and other corporations, religious and civil of that time.

Strong's translates the word as "orders of elders" or "estate of elders." Vines denote the meaning to be an assembly of aged men.

1. Therefore, the Council or Senate among the Jews **(Luke 22:66; Acts 22:5)**

2. Also, the elders and bishops in the local church…being raised up and qualified by the work of the Holy Spirit, and appointed to have spiritual care of and to exercise over sight over the churches. **(1 Timothy 4:14)**

3. "Presbuterion" has its root from the word "presbuteros" which, among things, denoted maturity of spiritual experience.

B. One could assume the following from the above scripture and information:

1. A presbyter is a "translocal" or "local" elder.

2. The presbytery is the coming together of the translocal and/or local elders to minister care and oversight to the spiritual needs of the local church.

II. SOME POSSIBLE SCRIPTURAL EXAMPLES OF THE PRESBYTERY FUNCTIONING

A. In **Acts 13:1-5** we find a group of prophets and teachers ministering unto the Lord.

1. This ministering is in the same vein as Samuel's service (**1 Samuel 3:1**) and is a religious function such as worship.

2. The Holy Spirit gave direction concerning certain individuals to be placed in ministry.

3. Presbytery action was taken by testing through prayer and confirming them by the laying on of hands.

B. In **Acts 15:1-34**, we find the apostles and elders at Jerusalem called upon to make spiritual discernment.

1. Paul's and Barnabas's work among the gentiles was being troubled by those who felt they must observe the Laws of Moses.

2. Both views were allowed to express themselves and testimony was given.

3. Presbytery action was taken by searching the scripture, waiting on the Holy Spirit, making discernment, and giving instruction.

III. THE PURPOSE OF THE PRESBYTERY COULD, THEREFORE BE AT LEAST TWO-FOLD

A. To confirm the Lord's will for candidates and to impart empowerment for their calling through the following expressions:

1. Prophecy, which in this case is a gift to the individual by the presbytery enabling their ministry and placement to be confirmed by Paul **(Acts 13:1-5)**. This is not to be confused with prophecy which is usually directed to the body and could be applied to several people **(1 Corinthians 14:3-4).**

2. Through the laying on of hands, which is a foundation stone **(Hebrews 6:2)** and the point of contact for the imparting of something from God **(1 Timothy 4:14).**

B. To make discernment on application of spiritual truths to given situations, opportunities, or needs, and share with the local congregation the findings and assist in carrying it out.

1. Through an understanding of the times and what ought to be done in relationship to them. (1 Chronicles 12:32; Luke 9:54- 56; John 4:21-23; 8:1-11)

2. Through and understanding of the culture involved and what expressions that would necessitate (Acts 15:5, 19- 24).

3. Through reaffirmation of biblical doctrine (Galatians 1:6-9)

IV. THE PRESBYTERY IS A MANIFESTATION OF GOD'S WISDOM

A. In propagating a healthy body.

1. If the body of Christ is healthy it will have a diversity of personalities, lifestyles, backgrounds, and concepts **(Matthew 28:19-20; 1 Corinthians 12-25).**

46

2. It will have the potential for being divisive over expressing one's faith in Christ **(Galatians 5:1; 13-15; 25-26; Ephesians 3, 4:1-4, 29-32)**

3. The presbytery is to share the wisdom of God in what the Body is to do to keep a harmonious witness. **(I Corinthians 12:14; 29-32)**

B. In giving insight and instruction to those called to serve.

1. Through sharing insights in matters of personal growth or testimony **(1 Timothy 4:6-16)**

2. Through sharing instruction on how the assembly can best function, what should be allowed and how things can be done **(1 Timothy, 2 Timothy, Titus)**

3. Being a personal source of encouragement to those who ministered. **(2 Timothy 1:3-11)**

The presbytery is of immeasurable help and importance to the corporate body and to individuals called to ministry. Just as a family must have clarification in many areas as it grows numerically and in maturity, so must the church. This usually ends up involving the parents (representing spiritual maturity and authority) using their God-given wisdom to give insight and supportive direction.

The Presbytery is parallel in the spiritual family---the church.

How important authority is in situations that demand answers and clarifications to keep the "family" functioning smoothly. Likewise, how important it is in the individual's life to have tangible affirmation of God's leading before entering ministry. If anything, the call to ministry intensifies the spiritual warfare in one's life and necessitates at times a very physical remembrance of encouragement (1 Timothy 1:18). Even Jesus, when he came to earth, went through a tangible affirmation process (Luke 2:25-38; Matthew 3:13-15). How important it is for us to function in a way befitting the children of God.

Chapter 12
Who Are You Joined To?

1 Corinthians 1:16-17

And I baptized also the household of Stephanas: besides, I know not whether I baptized any other. For Christ sent me not to baptize, but to preach the gospel: not with wisdom of words, lest the cross of Christ should be made of none effect.

Matthew 19:6

Wherefore they are no more twain, but one flesh. What therefore God hath joined together, let not man put asunder. He saith unto them, Moses because of the hardness of your hearts suffered you to put away your wives: but from the beginning it was not so.

1 Corinthians 1:10

Now I beseech you, brethren, by the name of our Lord Jesus Christ, that ye all speak the same thing, and that there be no divisions among you; but that ye be perfectly joined together in the same mind and in the same judgment.

1. Here are the principles that we gleaned from these scriptures above:

    A. **United in Vision:** like the people at the tower of Babel.

    B. **United in Sacrifice:** you can't have half of the people doing all the work, while the other half doesn't contribute at all.

    C. **United in Spirit:** you must corporately be knitted in heart and mind; not clones, but united in spirit.

Exodus 32:1

And when the people saw that Moses delayed to come down out of the mount, the people gathered themselves together unto Aaron, and said unto him, Up, make us gods, which shall go before us; for as for this Moses, the man that brought us up out of the land of Egypt, we know not what is become of him.

2 Timothy 2:2

And the things that thou hast heard of me among many witnesses, the same commit thou to faithful men, who shall be able to teach others also.

Proverbs 20:6

Most men will proclaim everyone his own goodness: but a faithful man who can find:

1 Samuel 13:6-13 - Self-will and joined the people.

When the men of Israel saw that they were in a strait, (for the people were distressed) then the people did hide themselves in caves, and in thickets, and in rocks, and in high places, and in pits. And Samuel said to Saul, thou has done foolishly: Thou hast not kept the commandment of the LORD thy God, which he commanded thee: for now would the LORD have established thy kingdom upon Israel forever.

1 Samuel 15:17- What in Saul?

And Samuel said, when thou wast little in thine own sight, wast thou not made the head of the tribe of Israel, and the LORD anointed thee king over Israel?

Number 25:3, 5

And Israel joined himself unto Baal-peor: and the anger of the LORD was kindled against Israel. And Moses said unto the judges of Israel, slay ye everyone his men that were joined unto Baal-peor.

Psalm 106: 28, 31

They joined themselves also unto Baal-peor, and ate the sacrifices of the dead. And that was counted unto him for righteousness unto all generations for evermore.

2. Six important facts about authority and power:

    a. All power is intended to operate under authority

    b. All authority comes from God

    c. Authority gives direction to power

    d. Authority sets boundaries for power

    e. Authority is God's plan to protect you

    f. Authority is God's vehicle to enable you to maximize your ability and potential

Chapter 13
Principles of Authority

Understanding Authority God's Way - Part I

Authority in the life of the church is vital to her existence. Unfortunately, our understanding of authority has been formed by society's definition. Since society is in a constant state of change, so are her definitions. Believers need to base their understanding of authority on God's Word, the Bible, not on society's role model.

I. WHAT IS AUTHORITY?

A. World Book Dictionary defines the word "authority" as follows:

1. The power to enforce obedience; right to control, command, or make right decisions, jurisdiction.

2. A person, body, board, or the like, that has such power, right or jurisdiction.

3. A source of correct information or wise advice: book or passage regarded as settling a disputed point.

4. An expert on some subject; person whose advice or opinion is accepted.

5. Power over the opinions of others; influence that commands respect and confidence.

6. Delegated power; authorization.

7. A judicial opinion that may be cited as a precedent.

8. Authority often implies legal power, given by a person's position or office, to give commands and enforce obedience: teachers have authority over pupils.

B. In the New Testament, the Greek uses several different words for authority[1].

   1. **"Exousia"**- *For I am a man under authority…* **(Matthew 8:9 KJV).** The word denotes delegated authority; a legal right.

   2. **"Katexousiazo"**- *You know that the rulers of the Gentiles lord it over them, and their great men exercise authority over them* **(Matthew 20:25 NASB).**

      A. The Greek word means "to have (yield) full privilege over."

      B. Jesus used the word twice **(Matthew 20:25 and Mark 10:42)** and both times it was in a negative sense.

   3. **"Aathenteo"**- *But I do not allow a woman to teach or exercise authority over a man, but to remain quiet* **(1 Timothy 2:12 NASB).**

      A. The Greek word means "to act of oneself and dominate by usurping authority."

         A. The sense seems to be that of manipulation for selfish reasons.

         B. When it comes to domination, manipulation, and usurping of authority, what Paul says about a women could also be said of a man.

   4. **"Huperoehe"**- (hoop-er-okh-ay')- *First of all, then I urge entreaties and prayers, petitions and thanksgivings, be made on behalf of all men, for kings and all who are in authority,* **(1 Timothy 2:1-2a NASB).**

---

1 All references are taken from the Strong's Exhaustive Concordance of the Bible

A. The Greek word carries a three-fold meaning: Prominence; superiority in rank or character; and excellency.

B. Examples of this type of authority would be: governmental authorities, church leadership in the body, and the presbytery.

C. Scripture clearly indicates various levels of authority.

   1. It is essential that a person always maintains a harmonious attitude with all levels of authority.

   2. God's divine will can be revealed to every believer individually; however, He often uses the wise counsel of those in authority over us.

   3. However, by resisting our authorities, we literally take upon ourselves consequences based on the degree of our resistance or rebellion. *Therefore, he who resists authority has opposed the ordinance of God; and they who have opposed will receive condemnation upon themselves.* **(Romans 13:2 NASB)**

II. THE PURPOSE OF AUTHORITY:

A. To develop the full potential of character.

   1. *And he went down with them, and came to Nazareth; and He continued in subjection to them; And Jesus kept increasing in wisdom and stature, and in favor with God and men.* **(Luke 2:51-51 NASB) Psalm 25; 14 Philippians 2:5-9**

B. To gain protection over temptation and destructive evil.

   1. *For rebellion is as the sin of witchcraft, and stubbornness is as iniquity and idolatry.* **(1 Samuel 15:23 KJV)**

      A. Both terms: "rebellion and witchcraft" have the same basic definition-subjecting oneself to the realm and power of Satan.

B. Remaining under the safeguards of authority instead of remaining under its dominance is the idea behind submitting to authority principle.

2. The godly are not preserved from temptation, but <u>delivered out</u> of them.

   A. *Then the Lord knows how to rescue the godly from temptation, and to keep the unrighteous under punishment for the day of judgment, and especially those who indulge the flesh in its corrupt desires and despise authority.* **(2 Peter 2:9-10a NASB)** (Note also verses 4-8)

   B. *No temptation has overtaken you.... God is faithful, who will not allow you to be tempted beyond what you are able; but with the temptation will provide the way of escape also, that you may be able to endure it.* **(1 Corinthians 10:13 NASB).**

   C. **James 1:2, 12-15**

   D. **Hebrews 4:14-16**

C. To discern and receive clear direction for life decisions.

1. Correct decisions are based on faith and listening to God: visualizing what God intends to do and having it clarified (and verified) by the authority structure you are accountable and responsible to.

   a. **Matthew 8:5-13** In verse ten, Jesus expressed this after the centurion indicated his understanding of authority structures. Our faith increases and stabilizes as we witness God speaking confirmation to us through those, He has placed in authority over us.

   b. **John 2:5** The first public miracle came as a direct request by His earthly mother, Mary. God used earthly authority to inaugurate the earthly ministry of Jesus.

2. **John 14:10-14** Jesus has power and glory to give because of His humility, respect, and submission to the authority of His Father, God.

D. To provide freedom to preach the Gospel.

1. **1 Timothy 2:1-2** Paul says that our motive for praying for those in authority is... *"that we may lead a tranquil and quiet life in all godliness and dignity."*

2. Paul, by life and witness, demonstrated that the driving force in his life was aggressive evangelism.

3. Governments concerning themselves with maintaining order and peace.

   a. To accomplish these goals, they must establish good lines of communication and transportation.

   b. These two are essential to mass evangelization.

III. THE STRUCTURES OF AUTHORITY:

A. Family Structure

1. Marriage of man and woman. It must be understood that in the sight of God, there is neither male nor female. However; to maintain order and unity in the home, each is given different responsibilities. These should never be taken as a justification of inequality or subservience.

   a. Husband to wife

      1. Man - **Genesis 2:24**
      2. *Rejoice in the wife of your youth*, **(Proverbs 5:18 NASB)**
      3. **Ephesians 5:25-26** Note that husbands are told three times to "love" their wives, while wives are only told once to submit.
      4. **1 Peter 3:7**
      5. **1 Timothy 2:8**

  6. **Let the husband fulfill his duty to his wife, (1 Corinthians 7:3-4 NASB)**

  7. **Ephesians 5:28**

 b. Wife to husband. Jesus (and the Apostle Paul) elevated the role of women far above that of society.

  1. *"Wives, be subject* ("Submit" KJV) *to your husbands, as to the Lord:* **(Ephesians 5:22 NASB).**

   a. The Greek word for "subject" (hupotasso) means to arrange under, to subject willingly, or to present.

   b. The key to understanding is in the last phrase: "as to the Lord."

2. **1 Peter 3:1-2** "Submissive" here means the same thing as **Ephesians 5:22**.

3. After Queen Vashti had been disrespectful to her husband, Xerxes, we read: "And when the king's edict...is heard throughout all his kingdom, great as it is, then all women will give honor to their husbands, great and small" **(Esther 1:20 NASB)**. This edict also led to the discovery of Esther as a replacement of Queen Vashti.

4. **Mark 10:9**

 c. Fathers (parents) to children; **Ephesians 6:4; Proverbs 22:6**

C. Parents should model these seven (7) characters qualities:

 1. A continual attitude of Gratefulness.

 2. A genuine spirit of Humility

 3. A true sense of Self-Control (emotions and tongue)

 4. Politeness with good manners. Total acceptance of each person.

5. Recognition of the personal potential and worth of each family member.

6. A mutual trust relationship which will earn the right to be heard.

d. Children to parents: **Ephesians 6:1-3, Proverbs 6:20-21, Colossians 3:20, Proverbs 30:17, Proverbs 15:5**

Children of any parent, are to be always respectful. Showing disrespect to a parent is also showing disrespect to God. This does not mean that parents are always right about everything, but it is a sin of rebellion to disrespect or slander. When parents are wrong (which happens often), learn to appeal to them when you feel your personal rights have violated.

Chapter 14

The Family

There cannot be too much emphasis given to the family unit. It is important and scriptural emphasis is second only to our personal relationship with the Lord Jesus. God's emphasis on the family permeates the scriptures. It is His primary organism of responsibility for the initial and on- going molding of individuals into His likeness and purpose. Much of God's eternal purpose for us rests on our proper understanding of all structuring of the home.

I. PURPOSE OF THE FAMILY

The creation of the physical family is recorded in the very beginning of the Bible. Father God instituted the family unit **(Genesis 2:18, 21-25)**:

    a. To have dominion (to tread down, subjugate, rule over) His creation.

    b. To procreate.

    c. To dress and keep His creation.

The creation of a spiritual family is recorded in the last book of the Bible.

    1. The Lord God will institute the eternal family unit **(Revelations 19:6-9)**.

2. He has commissioned this family unit.

   a. To assist in taking dominion **(Revelation 19:11-20;4).**

   b. To assist in ruling with His **(Revelation 3:21).**

Between these events, the family unit is to fulfill God's purpose in both realms.

1. The home is to exercise a physical dominion.

   a. Through work **(Proverbs 31:10-31; 2 Thessalonians 3:10-12; 1 Timothy 5:8).**

   b. Procreation in the marriage context **(Hebrews 13:4).**

   c. "Maintaining" of His purpose by obedience to His vision and our commitment **(Matthews 19: 1-15).**

2. The home is to exercise:

   a. Spiritual dominion through an eternal vision and purpose **(Deuteronomy 8:10-19)**

II. PROBLEMS WITH THE FAMILY UNIT

A. The family unit was created to function in a relationship with God.

   1. Mankind was commanded to feast on God's goodness **(Genesis 2:16).**

B. Government Structure-National, State, Local Officials, and Citizens **(Romans 13:1-5 and Peter 2:13-14).** When Daniel was asked by the king to do something that violated his conscience and convictions, he had a basis or right to appeal because he had always been respectful to the king even though he was a captive **(Daniel 1).** Therefore, it is a must that one is always respectful to government officials **(Romans 13;6-7).**

C. The Church Structure-Leaders and other church members. **(1 Thessalonians 5:12-13, Hebrews 13:17 and 1 Peter 5:1-3).** *Do not touch anointed ones and do my prophets no harm.* **(1 Chronicles 16:22 NASB).**

    a. There are grave consequences for rebelling against God's anointed ones **(Numbers 16).**

    b. Whether you agree or disagree with church leaders is not important, but what is of utmost urgency is that you always respectfully appeal when you disagree.

D. The Business Structure-Business Associates, Employers, and Fellow Employees **(Colossians 3:22-25, 1 Peter 2:18, and 1 Timothy 6:1-6).**

E. Structures are not the issue.

    1. The key to practical faith and direction is the ability to recognize what God is saying to you through the abilities, reactions, and directions of those who are responsible for various areas of your life.

    2. God is more concerned that your character is more like that of Jesus Christ than He is in which authority structure He uses to get his done.

    3. Therefore; if you push away (get out from under) the reproofs and authority of your parents, God only has to raise up another authority structure to put pressure on your resistance.

    4. Continued resistance ultimately leads to ruin. "A man who hardens his neck after much reproof will suddenly be broken beyond remedy." **(Proverbs 29:1 NASB).**

Chapter 15
Principles of Authority

Responding to Authority - Part II

The scriptures say, "But grow in grace and knowledge of our Lord and Savior Jesus Christ" … **(2 Peter 3:18 NASB)** The only way to grow in faith is to be in harmony with all <u>structures</u> of authority. Our response to authority be it righteous or unrighteous, will clearly reflect our level of spiritual maturity as well as determine the rate at which spiritual growth can occur.

I. WHY SOME RESIST AUTHORITY?

A. The basic causes of defying authority are: pride, ungratefulness, or a wounded spirit.

1. **Pride** - Lucifer rebelled because his heart was filled with pride **(Ezekiel 28: 12-17)**.

2. **Ungratefulness** - Adam and Eve disobeyed because they believed God was withholding something good from them **(Genesis 3:1-7)**.

3. **A Wounded Spirit** - Esau experienced a wounded spirit and therefore felt justified in rebelling against his father, God, and in plotting the murder of his brother **(Genesis 27:41; 28:6-9)**.

B. The temptation of Jesus was an attempt to cause Him to rebel against the authority of God the Father **(Matthew 4:1- 11 NASB)**.

    1. **Lust of the Eye**- (pride) Put on a reckless demonstration of power ... *If you are the Son of God, throw yourself down* ... (v.6)

    2. **Lust of the Flesh**- (Ungratefulness) Being ruled by your/our physical appetite and needs... *If you are the Son of God, command that these stones become bread.* (v.3)

    3. **Pride of Life**- (wounded spirit) Bypass the agony and shame of the cross... *All these things will I give You, if you would fall down and worship me.* (v.9)

C. Resisting or rebelling against authority is a sin.

    1. *"For rebellion is as the sin of divination* (witchcraft- KJV), *and insubordination is as iniquity and idolatry* **(1 Samuel 15:23 NASB)**.

    2. Confession and repentance bring forgiveness **(1 John 1:9)**.

II. RESPONSIBILITY AND ACCOUNTABILITY OF HOW TO WISELY APPEAL TO AUTHORITY:

A. No matter how inconsistent or unfair those in authority may be, as believers in Jesus Christ, we are responsible for our responses to them.

    1. God can and does use those who are hardest to get along with to motivate us to develop mature attitudes.

    2. God is not nearly as concerned with what we go through as He is with our response to those individuals and circumstances.

        a. In all that God designs or allows us to experience, His primary concern is that our attitudes become consistent with those of His Son, Jesus Christ.

        b. "Although He was a Son, He learned obedience from the things which He suffered." **(Hebrews 5:8 NASB)**

B. Learning to understand what those in authority are trying to achieve is essential.

    1. Make sure you know their basic intentions. Sometimes our perceptions are wrong.

    2. Daniel, with a mature, respectful attitude, discovered that the King's command to eat certain food was to make him healthy and wise. Because he had a proper view of his authority's intention, Daniel had a basis upon which to appeal, offering on a test basis an alternative diet that would not violate his personal convictions.

III. SEVEN REQUIREMENTS FOR OFFERING AN EFFECTIVE APPEAL

A. You must be in "Right Standing."

    1. Have you put yourself under God's authority by receiving Jesus Christ as your Savior and Lord? **(Romans 10:9-13)**

    2. Do you have an open two-way communication (fellowship) with God by confessing all known sin to God and entering into Christ's victory over the power and appeal of sin? **(Romans 6; 8:1-15)**

    3. Are you under God-given authority?

        a. What would any of your past or present authorities indicate has been your attitude towards them? **(Ephesians 6:1-9)**

        b. Do you have a clear conscience with all structures of authority? **(Romans 13:7)**

        c. Have you fulfilled all your responsibilities to the authority that you are now planning an appeal? **(1 Samuel 15:22)**

B. You must have "Right Motives"

    1. The authority who listens to your appeal will quickly sense whether it is prompted by selfish motives or by genuine concern for his welfare.

2. An effective appeal grows out of right motives. It communicates three vital concerns that you should have for your human authorities.

    a. Concern for his reputation

        Jesus taught to guard reputations by praying, *Hallowed be Thy name* **(Matthew 6:9 NASB) Proverbs 22:1**

    b. Concerns for his goals

        It is your responsibility to know what your authority's goals are and help him achieve them if they are in harmony with Scripture. *Thy kingdom come ....* **(Matthew 6:10 NASB)**. Here Jesus clearly is focusing attention on the importance of basing one's appeal on the goals of the one being petitioned.

C. Concern for his authority

1. Anyone in a position of responsibility will be alert to those who challenge his authority.

    a. *"Thy will be done, on earth as it is in heaven"* **(Matthew 6:10 NASB)**. Here Jesus conveyed the importance of relating your petition to the authority of the one whom you are appealing.

    b. *"For Thine is the kingdom, and the power, and glory, forever Amen."* **(Matthew 6:13 NASB)**. Jesus emphasized that we are to be committed to the success of our authorities. This demonstrates a servant's spirit which is essential to finding favor with God or with human authorities.

2. If a leader is robbed of that authority, he will be unable to fulfill his responsibility.

3. You must recheck your motives.

    a. Is your real concern to protect your reputation or the reputation of God and your authorities?

b. Can you base your appeal on helping your authorities become successful in God's eyes by being wise leaders, protectors, and providers? **(Hebrews 10:24)**

c. When you make your appeal, are you doing it so that your authorities can give a good account to God for the way that they have used their authority? **(Hebrews 13:17)**

D. You must appeal at the "Appropriate Time." There are three basic factors that determine whether your appeal is being made at the right time:

1. Is your authority free to concentrate on your appeal? Ask permission for full attention before appealing.

2. Will your authority see that you are ready to sacrifice for your appeal? A person in authority will often weigh a request by how much you are willing to sacrifice for it.

3. Will your authority know that you are ready to accept whatever decision is given? An authority must know that he has the freedom to make the decision. He should not feel that it has already been made for him. Neither should our appeal cause him to feel under pressure.

E. You must give "Accurate Information" There are three areas of information which must be accurate if your appeal is to be effective.

1. The first involves information about yourself. You must accurately assess your strengths and weaknesses and discern where these will have a bearing on your appeal.

2. The second involves the accuracy of the information in your appeal. If the person to whom you are appealing knows that you are unaware of important facts or are ignoring them, he will certainly have a negative outlook toward your petition.

3. The third aspect of an appeal requires accurate information about the one to whom you are appealing. You must know how your petition will relate to the background, interests, and viewpoints of your authority.

F. You must have the "Right Attitudes." The major reason appeals are rejected is because of wrong attitudes.

1. When one under authority makes an appeal with a wrong attitude, the one in authority may never really hear what is being said. He may be more concerned about the wrong attitudes than about the merits of the petition.

2. *And forgive us our debts, as we forgive our debtors,* (**Matthew 6:12 KJV**). Christ required that you have the right attitude before you will be able to wisely petition.

3. The attitudes of reverence, loyalty, and gratefulness is essential to an effective appeal. However; you must first remove the negative attitudes of rebellion and resignation which are sinful.

    a. Lay Aside Rebellion and Resignation

    1. Rebellion- You may be obedient outwardly and yet have a spirit of rebellion. This spirit will manifest itself by the number, the purpose, the manner, the length, and the spirit of your appeals.

    2. Resignation- This attitude is of equal danger because it amounts to blind obedience. When you act in blind obedience, you cease to think for yourself or take personal responsibility for the actions you are told to carry out. Every command must be evaluated on the basis of God's moral law. Never violate God's truth

b. The Attitude of Reverence

1. Reverence is the result of recognizing that God works through human authorities. It comes by separating an authority's divine position from his human personality.

2. The factors which may cause an authority not to react negative to an appeal are: respect shown to him as a person and reverence for his position under God.

3. Definition - The knowledge that God is shaping me into the likeness of Christ through the people and experiences in my life **(Proverbs 23:17-18)**.

c. The Attitude of Loyalty

1. Loyalty is the one-character quality most looked for and appreciated by those in positions of authority.

2. Loyalty is the fruit of a servant's heart- an inward motivation to make the ones whom you are serving successful.

3. Definition - Using difficult times to remind me of my dedication to those who God has asked me to help **(John 15:13)**.

4. Appeals that arise out of a loyal spirit and a servant's heart have an entirely different tone than those which come from a disloyal, selfish spirit.

d. The Attitude of Gratefulness

1. Human authorities tend to reward those who are grateful, but react quickly and coldly to the ungrateful person.

2. Gratefulness is built on recognizing and admiring what those in authority have done.

3. A lack of gratefulness results in negative outlook. That negative outlook is interpreted by those in authority as rejection and condemnation of what they have done or have not done.

4. A grateful spirit is only possible after you give God all your expectations and recognize that whatever He gives is really more than you deserve.

5. Make **Psalm 62:5** your daily motto: *My soul, wait only upon God and silently submit to Him; for my hope and expectation are from Him* (**AMP**).

G. You must use "Appropriate Words

1. To avoid unnecessary reactions, choose words that will guide important ideas around the mental roadblocks of your listeners.

2. Often, the very nature of an appeal is going to go against the intentions of this authority. Therefore, it is extremely easy for your words to be misunderstood.

    a. The right words are gracious words.

    b. They are humble words, free of resentment and arrogance.

    c. They must not be inflammatory.

3. Scripture emphasizes the importance of using right words when making an appeal to one in authority.

    a. *He who loves purity of heart and whose speech is gracious, the king is his friend.* (**Proverbs 22:11 NASB**)

    b. **Proverbs 10:11, 13, 19, 20, 31-32**

H. You must display the "Right Response If Your Appeal Is Rejected."

1. The ultimate test of your true attitude is seen in your response to an appeal that has been turned down.

2. A gracious response will not only give a proper testimony, but it may also prompt the one who has turned down your appeal to reconsider.

a. This should not be seen as manipulative technique for ultimately getting your own way.

b. It will however; cause your authority to be more open to future appeals which you may need to make.

c. If your appeal is accepted, you also have an obligation to demonstrate a right spirit; genuine gratitude.

Every person encounters authority structures in one way or another. Frequently there are unresolved conflicts and hurts. When these painful experiences become part of your soul's memories, they begin to alter your habits and responses to the structure of authority. This results in a distorted view of not only earthly authority structures, but also your understanding of God's rightful authority and influence in your life.

Therefore, you must be in harmony with all structures of authority. Where there is hurt, seek healing through Christ. Where there is bitterness and sin, repent. Seek reconciliation in broken, strained relationships. It is the only way to grow in your faith and in God's grace.

Chapter 16
The Local Congregation

Flock

The local church, as it congregates, is a miracle in progress. It is the coming together of individuals birthed by the Holy Spirit through Christ (**1 Corinthians 12:12-13**) for the purpose of glorifying God. It is also true when two or more people gather, there is potential for problems due to differing opinions, motivations, and/or purposes.

With Satan's encouragement, divisions can result that causes the local church to be a stumbling block instead of a glory to God, the purpose of this teaching is to help each of us to discern what type of relationship we have to the local church.

Figurative speech (not necessarily scripturally based) is used to help us see clearly our attitudes and actions and their resulting affect. In no way is it meant to belittle those who might see disruptively patterns toward the Body in their lives, but to bring to focus the seriousness of purpose concerning the Body of Christ.

I. THE LOCAL CHURCH

A. The word for "church" comes from the Greek "ekklesia" and means "a calling out of orcongregation." It therefore does not refer to a building but to a people or assembly of people who:

1. Acknowledge Jesus as "Christ, the Son of the Living God" (**Matthew 16:16**).

2. Under the conviction of the Holy Spirit, identifies with and continues in Christ **(Acts 2:38-47)**.

3. Follow the call and cause of Christ **(John 10:9, 24-27)**.

4. Experienced spiritually the new birth in Christ **(1 Corinthians 13:12-13)**.

5. Have a willingness to suffer for the church **(Colossians 1:24)**.

B. The "church" is to be seen as:

1. Christ's body **(Ephesians 1:22-23; Colossians 1:18)**.

2. An inhabitation of God as it assembles **(Ephesians 2:19-22)**.

3. The church and the local congregation are figuratively referred to as a "flock" **(John 10:16; 1 Peter 5:2)**.

II. THE SHEEP

A. Sheep are representative of those in the local church who are obedient, dedicated, and fruitful to the Lord in their setting **(Matthew 10:16-27)**.

1. They realize God likens all of us to sheep and He does not want us to perish **(Isaiah 53:4-7)**.

2. They find their satisfaction in being a sheep unto the Lord Jesus **(Psalm 23:1)**.

B. Their characteristics are:

1. They love to be led **(John 10:27)**.

   a. The sheep's nature is such that they are to be led, not driven.

   b. Sheep represent persons willing to be led.

71

2. They love to lie down in green pastures **(Psalm 23:2)**.

   a. Sheep have a need to find and partakes of food before they rest.

   b. Sheep represent persons who desire to be at local assemblies to feed upon the Word of God.

3. They love the still waters **(Psalm 23:2)**.

   a. Sheep detest agitated waters and refuse to drink from them.

   b. Sheep represent persons who shy away from and refuse to participate in strife, doctrinal debate, arguing, dissension, or derogatory conversations.

4. They are known for their wool **(Proverbs 27:26)**.

   a. Sheep grow wool naturally and love shearing time. It is a time of "lightening" their load.

   b. Sheep represent those who find joyfulness in giving of time and material goods **(2 Corinthians 8:7-9; 9:7)**.

   c. The need of sheep:

      1. To <u>KNOW</u> the voice of the shepherd **(John 10:1-15, 27; Jeremiah 3:15)**.

      2. To <u>FOLLOW</u> the shepherd **(1 Corinthians 11:1; 1 Thessalonians 1:5-6)**.

      3. To <u>EAT</u> what the shepherd ministers from the Word **(2 Timothy 2: 1-2; 1 Peter 5:2)**.

      4. To <u>HEED</u> the warnings of the shepherd **(2 Timothy 4:2-4)**.

      5. To <u>BEAR</u> fruit **(John 15:16)**.

      6. To <u>ALLOW</u> the shepherd to shear **(Ephesians 4:11-16)**.

III. THE GOATS

A. Goats are representative of those in the local church who usually end up involved in undercurrents or dissensions without necessarily meaning to.

1. They consider themselves to be and are a part of the flock **(Proverbs 27:23-26)**.

2. They have the "ability" to give some value (in form of "milk"), but not to the full potential of the rest of the flock **(Proverbs 27:26-27)**.

B. Their characteristics are:

1. They are harder to lead than sheep.

   a. Goats by nature are more suspicious than sheep. They have a tendency to buck or stand apart.

   b. Persons who have such a weakness, have a tendency to be caught up into an opposition opinion of what is trying to be established, "fault finding" (with their shepherd, pastures, waters) and in backbiting (butting). They can become blind to this through their own stubbornness **(Psalm 105:14-15; Ephesians 5:21; Galatians 5:13-13)**.

2. They are harder to satisfy than sheep

   a. Goats are not satisfied with "surface findings" they want to get to the root of things. There is a tendency to become agitated over feeding habits and techniques. They can be known for eating almost anything that comes in their path.

   b. Persons who have such a weakness usually end up in an agitated state with the leadership and Body associated with the efforts to get the "truth" **(2 Thessalonians 3:1-6; 1 Timothy 6:1-6)**.

C. The need of goats:

1. To <u>SEE</u> the discontent and divisiveness that this nature brings into the flock because "like produces like" **(James 3:13; 4:5)**.

2. To <u>CHOOSE</u> to become as a sheep unto the Lord **(James 4:6-10)**.

3. To <u>UNDERSTAND</u> the blessings of becoming a Lamb of God. **(John 10:28-29; Matthew 25:33-40; John 21:15-17)**.

IV. THE WOLVES

A. Wolves are representative of those who would come into the local church and cause grievous and damaging consequences to the local assembly **(John 6:70-71)**.

1. They do not belong to the flock of God **(Acts 20:29)**.

2. They will try to conceal themselves and deceive others into believing they belong **(Matthew 7:15; 1 John 2:19)**.

3. Their motives are impure whether they are aware of it or not **(Acts 20:30)**.

B. Their characteristics are:

1. They seek the high places so they can eye their prey.

   a. Wolves <u>desire</u> to get above or on a higher level than their prey so they can eventually get to the sheep.

   b. Persons who fall into this category desire all the authority and positions they can get. It is not for the purpose of being responsible to God, but to satisfy some inward need, hunger, or desire **(Zephaniah 3: 3-4; Ezekiel 34:7-10)**

2. They are sly and sneaky.

    a. Wolves are deceptive and will do their best to stay away from the shepherds' gaze and yet cling to the sheep.

    b. Persons with wolfish attributes will try to discredit leadership and make themselves acceptable in the congregation's eyes. They will focus on the "wrongs" or shortcomings of the flock due to the leadership's "weaknesses," yet be verbally supportive of leadership in their presence; they thrive on symptoms of carnality, strife, and sin in a church setting **(Jude 10-19)**.

3. They show their teeth and growl. Sheep and goats do not.

    a. Wolves are meat-eaters and show that trait by their willingness to devour.

    b. Persons who are functioning in this manner can manifest a carnal, strifeful, harsh, unsubmissive, or resentful spirit **(2 Timothy 2: 24-26)**.

    c. The need of wolves:

        1. To REPENT of one's sins **(Matthew 7:15-23)**.

        2. To CONFESS of your need for Christ and come under His Lordship **(Matthew 7:21)**.

        3. To RESIST the inward drive for a high position in the church and serve basic needs that come before you **(Matthew 20:25-28)**.

        4. To DEAL with resentment toward or desire to defame Pastors/Elders/Leadership by submitting to them **(Hebrews 13:17)**.

        5. To FLEE opportunities to create strife or draw disciples after yourself **(Galatians 6:3-10)**.

V. SHEEPDOGS

A. Sheepdogs are representative of those from within the congregation who are called to be elders, guards, or watchmen to the flock (**Acts 20:28-31**).

    1. They are called and equipped by the Lord through His channels (**Acts 14:23**).

    2. They are to protect and care for the flock under the encouragement of the Apostolic Trans Local Leadership (**1 Peter 5:1-3**).

B. Their characteristics are:

    1. They work in <u>cooperation</u> with the shepherd.

        a. Sheepdogs will strategically position themselves on the perimeters of the flock to keep the sheep together, corral the goats, and drive off the wolves (**Acts 20:28-31**).

        b. Persons called to this purpose will have a love for the flock of God and will desire to care for it (**1 Peter 5:2**).

    2. They work the sheep toward the Pastor instead of away from him.

        a. A sheepdog does not presume to guard the sheep from the shepherd, but to guard the sheep "for" the shepherd,

        b. A person functioning in this capacity will refrain from working against others in leadership and encourage the flock to not to be divisive (**1 Corinthians 1:10-16; 3:1-10**).

    3. They do not or dare not get a taste for "lamb"

        a. A sheepdog who gets a taste for flesh and blood no longer can function, because he has become like a wolf.

        b. Persons called to function in the oversight capacity must always have the pure motive to please the Lord and get their encouragement from Him, not from the sheep (**1 Pet. 5:3-4**).

C. The need of sheepdogs:

1. To WATCH over the sheep, and watch out for wolves **(1 Corinthians 16:13-16).**

2. To <u>RECEIVE</u> instruction from you Shepherd **(1 Corinthians 4:6-21).**

3. To <u>AQUIRE</u> a taste to serve and not to savor "lamb" **(John 13:12-17).**

4. To <u>KEEP</u> a short remembrance of the pastor's and people's shortcomings or sins that are confessed **(Matthew 18:21-35).**

How we all need to examine ourselves in light of the Lord's purpose for the Body of Christ! If one's attitude, performance, or characteristics are different than that portrayed by the sheep, we need to humbly admit it and allow for a working of God's grace in our lives.

We need to come under His Lordship in the Body of Christ instead of trying to leave it or destroy it. By doing so, we create an atmosphere for a great working of the Lord.

Contact us:

www.christbiblediscipleship.com

apostledavidallen53@yahoo.com

Williamyoho1959@gmail.com

Made in the USA
Columbia, SC
22 January 2024

29893116R00050